陕西省非物质文化遗产名录中的民俗文化英译

陕西省社会科学基金项目（2015K025）研究成果
陕西省教育厅科学研究计划项目（16JK1731）研究成果
国家社会科学基金项目（19XYY006）阶段性成果

陕西省文化和旅游厅
陕西省非物质文化遗产保护中心 编

苏蕊 译
罗宾·吉尔班克 审校

AN ENGLISH GUIDE TO SHAANXI
INTANGIBLE FOLK CULTURE

西北大学出版社
·西安·

图书在版编目（CIP）数据

陕西省非物质文化遗产名录中的民俗文化英译：汉英对照 / 苏蕊译. —西安：西北大学出版社，2021.11
ISBN 978-7-5604-4864-0

Ⅰ. ①陕… Ⅱ. ①苏… Ⅲ. ①风俗习惯—介绍—陕西—汉、英 Ⅳ. ①K892.441

中国版本图书馆 CIP 数据核字（2021）第 230048 号

陕西省非物质文化遗产名录中的民俗文化英译：汉英对照
SHAANXISHENG FEIWUZHI WENHUA YICHAN MINGLU ZHONG DE MINSU WENHUA YINGYI : HANYING DUIZHAO

陕西省文化和旅游厅　陕西省非物质文化遗产保护中心　编
苏　蕊　译

出版发行　西北大学出版社
（西北大学校内　邮编：710069　电话：029-88302621　88303593）
http: //nwupress.nwu.edu.cn　　E-mail: xdpress@nwu.edu.cn

经　　销	全国新华书店	
印　　刷	西安华新彩印有限责任公司	
开　　本	787 毫米×1092 毫米　1/16	
印　　张	15	
版　　次	2021 年 11 月第 1 版	
印　　次	2021 年 11 月第 1 次印刷	
字　　数	239 千字	
书　　号	ISBN 978-7-5604-4864-0	
定　　价	36.00 元	

本版图书如有印装质量问题，请拨打 029-88302966 予以调换。

血社火
Bloody Dumb Show

叶子
Yezi

正月里耍社火	In lunar January, we stage our parade
个子碎 我站在人前头	I, a tiny scrap, stand before the villagers
队长说 把这小子绑了	The troupe leader barks: "Fasten that little kid up"
几个娃娃伙高高过来	A couple of painted dolls totter over
给我安装上木腿	To equip me with wooden splints
我说 我不会走路	I protest at how I can't stilt walk
队长说 不行	The old man insists that I can
我说 我真的不会走路	"I really cannot do it," I plead
队长看我额颅上冒汗 就说	He fixes me, my brow now beaded
那就装死狗	"Then play the mutt that's for the chop"
几个娃娃伙过来把我的腿卸了	Some other dolls mince over, these legs are detached
我坐在墙上	I perch on the wall
他们端着颜料跳来跳去	A cluster encircling with greasepaint
围住给我画脸谱	Then outline the facial design
好了么 我问	"Looks OK?" I ask

别说话	"Don't grumble about this stuff"
过了一阵阵我又问 好了么	A while later I query: "Fine now?"
画歪了你赔呀	"The makeup mustn't appear skew-whiff"
我叫人家架到三奔子上	I am hoisted onto the tricycle
低头	"Bow your head"
我低头	I lower my crown
不准动弹	"Keep still"
我不动弹 就这么	This body is motionless. That's the point
三奔子跟在锣鼓后头	The trike shudders along behind the drummer
锣鼓跟在秧歌后头	Gongs and drums tail the *yangge* troupe
一路上吹吹打打	Blowing and blasting the whole route long
到了政府门口 镇长笑着放炮	Until at the town office gate, the chortling headman sets firecrackers alight
说了些表扬的话 也可能	Praise is audible, perhaps
说了些批评的话	A chill of criticism, too
我看见队长点头哈腰	I can see the troupe leader bend and bow
他们朝三奔子望着	All eyes are on the tricycle
这个额颅上镶着一把斧头的人	And the player with the hatchet stroking his brow
有人指指点点	Some shocked fingers point
有人说我死了	Some are adamant I've been slain
有个碎娃娃捂住眼睛	A little kid covers his eyes
我认为很成功	I think it's worked
我一动不动	I do not twitch

(Translated by Robin Gilbank and Su Rui)

Introduction

Spring Festival, or Chinese New Year, is ubiquitous as a subject of art and literature. Foreigners who have never set foot in China may yet be familiar with traditions like eating boiled dumplings, hanging lanterns to burn overnight, and lighting firecrackers. Less well known are the carnivalesque outdoor performances which proliferate in the countryside around central Shaanxi. Called *Shehuo* in Chinese, the literal meaning of the name is "social fire", a phrase sufficiently ambiguous to raise confusion. Although far from concise "folk acrobatic and pyrotechnic performance" better conveys the fact that this is a celebration involving the community and entailing dramatic, even perilous, spectacle.

While working on the translation of this book, I stumbled upon the Baoji writer Yezi's poem on this subject. Remarkably, it is told in the first person from the perspective of a child made to play one of the "dolls" performing in the parade. He is at first handed a pair of stilts and, having no experience of walking with elongated legs, refuses. As a consequence, he winds up drawing the short straw and being made to play a figure who is violently killed. The poem does not elucidate the exact content of the drama, though one can sense the trepidation of the boy being hoisted up onto the precarious rig. Indeed the reaction of many who watch *Shehuo* for the first time is to question how the child performers manage to remain balanced on what see like too fine and fragile a scaffold? Is it reinforced with steel? Are the "dolls" mannequins or mysteriously inanimate people?

The boy actor's fear is not confined to the risk of injury. The troupe leader is brusque and surly, so the junior player could easily come in for a scolding should he move or blink after the fatal blow is dealt. This may be entertaining for spectators, though the participants are reminded that they also bear the weight of their ancestral tradition and nothing, from the makeup to the manoeuvres, must be allowed to run awry.

As is detailed in the present book, *Shehuo* come in diverse forms, their variation being attributable to the histories and cultures of the local community. In Houguanzhai, Chang'an District, the spectacle features the semi-comical riding of a farmyard cow, whereas in Pucheng the menfolk simulate gore-soaked mock bouts of combat. Onlookers may laugh or marvel or be feel sick to their stomach. Unfortunately, as participants die off and popular interests change future generations may not feel assured of being able to share in these centuries' old customs. Hence, to produce a book outlining the design and format of these specimens of intangible folk culture is both a timely and valuable project.

The subject matter also extends to encompass how historical figures like the Yellow Emperor, the Fire Emperor, Sima Qian, and Sun Simiao are commemorated in places in Shaanxi associated with them. It includes subject matter as varied as temple fairs, matrimonial rites, dragon boat racing and gastronomy. In many cases, the reader is made to appreciate how climate, topography and even the local dialect have interacted to spawn a vibrant culture. This effect is further vivified by a range of original illustrations created by Mathew Russell.

Robin Gilbank

English Department,

Northwest University,

Xi'an, Shaanxi, China

目录
Contents

1 陕西省第一批非物质文化遗产名录中的民俗
The Folk Culture in the First Batch of the Intangible Cultural Heritage in Shaanxi Province ·· 1

1.1 黄帝陵祭典
The Worship Ceremony at the Yellow Emperor Mausoleum ············ 3

1.2 宝鸡民间社火
The Folk *Shehuo* Performance in the Baoji Area ························ 7

1.3 药王山庙会
The Mount Yaowang Temple Fair ·· 12

1.4 延川小程村原生态民俗文化
The Original Ecological Folk Culture of Xiaocheng Village in Yanchuan County ·· 14

1.5 骊山女娲补天
Nüwa Mends the Sky at Mount Li ·· 17

1.6 长武道场
The Taoist Rite in Changwu County ··· 19

1.7 炎帝陵祭典
The Worship Ceremony at the Mausoleum of the Yan Emperor ·········· 22

1.8 司马迁民间祭祀
Venerating Sima Qian ·· 25

1.9 东庄神楼
The Deity Tower in Dongzhuang Village ······································ 28

1.10 尧山圣母庙会
  The Holy Mother Temple Fair at Mount Yao ················ 30

1.11 蒲城血故事特技
  The Pucheng Bloody Dumb Show ······················ 32

1.12 谷雨祭祀文祖仓颉典礼
  Grain-Rain Day Veneration of Cang Jie, the Inventor of Chinese Characters
  ·· 34

1.13 白云山庙会
  The Mount Baiyun Temple Fair ······················· 36

1.14 洋县悬台社火艺术
  The *Shehuo* Performance on Suspended Stages in Yang County ········ 39

1.15 安康市汉滨区龙舟风俗
  Dragon Boat Racing in Hanbin District, Ankang City ············ 41

1.16 延安老醮会
  Ancient Sacrificial Rituals in Yan'an ···················· 43

1.17 长安王曲城隍庙祭祀和庙会
  The City God Temple Sacrificial Ceremony and Temple Fair at Wangqu Street in Chang'an District ·························· 46

1.18 侯官寨迎春社火牛老爷
  The *Shehuo* Performance for Receiving the Lord Niu in Houguanzhai Village
  ·· 47

1.19 栎阳马踏青器山社火
  The *Shehuo* Performance of Paper Horses Striding on a Porcelain Mountain in Yueyang Town ································· 49

1.20 户县社火
  The *Shehuo* Performance in Hu County ·················· 51

1.21 蒋村正月民俗活动
  The Folk Custom Activities in the First Lunar Month in Jiang Village ··· 52

1.22 陇州社火
  The *Shehuo* Performance in Longzhou ·················· 54

1.23 东峪孝歌
  The Mourning Song of Dongyu ······················· 56

1.24 铁里芯子
Tieli *Xinzi* ·· 57

1.25 陈炉窑神庙春秋祭祀礼仪
The Spring and Autumn Sacrificial Rites at the Chenlu Kiln Temple······ 59

1.26 耀州火亭子
The Fire Pavilion in the Yaozhou Area ·································· 61

1.27 勉县武侯墓清明祭祀活动
The Qingming Sacrificial Rite at the Wuhou Temple in Mian County ··· 63

2 陕西省第二批非物质文化遗产名录中的民俗
The Folk Culture in the Second Batch of the Intangible Cultural Heritage in Shaanxi Province ···65

2.1 西安都城隍庙民俗
Folk Custom at the Xi'an Metropolitan City God Temple ··············· 67

2.2 西安大白杨社火芯子
The *Shehuo* Performance on *Xinzi* in Grand Baiyang Village, Xi'an City ··· 69

2.3 户县北乡迎祭城隍民俗活动
The City God Collection and Veneration Ceremony in Northern Hu County ·· 71

2.4 楼观台祭祀老子礼仪
The Sacrificial Etiquette for the Veneration of Laozi at Louguantai Temple in Zhouzhi County ·· 75

2.5 华夏财神故里祭祀活动
The Sacrificial Activities to Worship the God of Wealth in His Hometown ·· 77

2.6 渭河南忙罢古会
The Ancient Slack-Season Gathering of Kith and Kin on the South Bank of the River Wei ·· 81

2.7 长武庙宇泥塑礼仪
The Monastic Clay Sculptures of Changwu County ··············· 83

2.8 蒲城罕井秋千民俗

The Swing Custom of Hanjing Town in Pucheng County ········· 85

2.9 渭北细狗撵兔竞技
The Contest of Chasing Rabbits with Greyhounds from North of the River Wei ·· 88

2.10 跑骡车
Driving Mule Carts ··· 91

2.11 华阴司家秋千会
The Sijia Swing Fair in Huayin City ························· 93

2.12 蕴空山庙会
The Mount Yunkong Temple Fair ···························· 96

2.13 医陶始祖与雷公庙会
The Sage of Ceramics and Pharmacology and Leigong Temple Fair ······ 98

2.14 香山庙会
The Fragrant Mountain Temple Fair ······················· 101

2.15 安塞转九曲
Walking the 9-Twist Maze of Lanterns in Ansai County ············ 104

2.16 横山牛王会
The Niuwang Fair in Hengshan County ················· 106

2.17 南郑协税社火高跷
The Xieshui Stilt-Walking *Shehuo* Performance in Nanzheng County ··· 109

2.18 谷雨公祭仓颉仪式
The Grain-Rain Day Official Worship Ceremony for Cang Jie ············ 111

2.19 丹凤高台芯子
The *Shehuo* Performance on High Platform *Xinzi* in Danfeng County ··· 113

3 陕西省第三批非物质文化遗产名录中的民俗
The Folk Culture in the Third Batch of the Intangible Cultural Heritage in Shaanxi Province ·· 117

3.1 上巳节风俗
The Customs of Shangsi Festival ······························ 119

3.2 终南山钟馗信仰民俗

The Customs for Worshipping Zhong Kui in the Zhongnan Mountains ······ 123

3.3 西王禹村纸台

The Paper Platform of Xiwangyu Village ··· 127

3.4 渭城区二月二古庙会

The Ancient Temple Fair on the Lunar February 2nd in Weicheng District ··· 130

3.5 彬县灯山庙会

The Mount Lamp Temple Fair in Bin County ·· 133

3.6 姜嫄庙会

The Jiang Yuan Temple Fair ·· 136

3.7 灵山庙会

The Mount Lingshan Temple Fair ··· 139

3.8 龙门洞庙会

The Longmen Cave Temple Fair ·· 141

3.9 二月二庙会

The Lunar February 2nd Temple Fair ·· 146

3.10 鱼河堡府城隍庙庙会

The Prefect City God Temple Fair in Yuhebu Village ······························ 148

3.11 无量山莲云寺庙会

The Lianyun Temple Fair on Mount Wuliang ··· 152

3.12 延安太和山庙会

The Mount Taihe Temple Fair at Yan'an ··· 154

3.13 宁陕城隍庙会

The Ningshan City God Temple Fair ·· 156

3.14 彬县大佛寺三月八庙会

The Big Buddha Temple Fair on Lunar March 8th in Bin County ············ 159

3.15 苏蕙织锦回文与武功民间送手绢风俗

Su Hui Brocading Palindrome Poems on Silk and the Folk Custom of Sending Handkerchiefs as Gifts in Wugong County ··· 162

3.16 重阳追节送花糕

Giving Courtesy Steamed Buns as Gifts at Double Ninth Festival ············ 163

3.17 大荔乞巧节

The Qiqiao Festival in Dali County ·· 166

3.18 大荔血故事
　　The Bloody Dumb Show in Dali County ·················· 169

3.19 华山红社火
　　The Mount Hua Bloody *Shehuo* Performance ············ 171

3.20 定边赛驴会
　　The Dingbian Donkey Race Fair ························· 175

3.21 绥德定仙墕娘娘庙花会
　　The Niangniang Temple Flower Fair in Dingxianyan Village, Suide County
　　·· 177

3.22 志丹过大年
　　Passing the Year in Zhidan County ····················· 180

3.23 沿门子
　　Yanmenzi (Door-to-Door *Yangge* Dance Team Paying New Year's Visit)
　　·· 183

3.24 洛川婚俗
　　The Wedding Customs of Luochuan County ·········· 186

3.25 陕北丧葬习俗
　　Burial Customs of Northern Shaanxi ··················· 188

3.26 洛川灯会
　　The Luochuan Lantern Fair ····························· 190

3.27 扫五穷
　　Sweeping Away the Five Poverties ····················· 193

3.28 商南花灯
　　The Festive Lanterns of Shangnan County ············ 195

4 陕西省第四批非物质文化遗产名录中的民俗
The Folk Culture in the Fourth Batch of the Intangible Cultural Heritage in Shaanxi Province ··· 197

4.1 蒲城芯子
　　The *Xinzi* Performance in the Pucheng Area ········· 199

4.2 船张芯子

　　　　The Chuanzhang Village *Xinzi* Performance ·············· 200

4.3 二曲礼仪

　　　　Erqu Etiquette ·············· 203

4.4 关中丧葬风俗

　　　　Funeral Customs in the Guanzhong Area ·············· 205

4.5 麟游地台社火

　　　　The Ground-Stage *Shehuo* Performance in the Linyou Area·············· 207

4.6 太白高芯社火

　　　　The Taibai *Shehuo* Performance on a High *Xinzi* ·············· 210

4.7 华山庙会

　　　　The Mount Hua Temple Fair ·············· 213

4.8 吴堡黄河古渡

　　　　The Yellow River Ancient Ferry in Wubu County ·············· 215

4.9 柞水十三花

　　　　The 13-Blossom Banquet in Zhashui County ·············· 217

4.10 漫川古镇双戏楼庙会

　　　　The Twin-Theatre Temple Fair at the Ancient Town of Manchuan ·········· 219

Acknowledgements ·············· 222

1 陕西省第一批
非物质文化遗产名录中的民俗

The Folk Culture in the
First Batch of the Intangible Cultural
Heritage in Shaanxi Province

1.1 黄帝陵祭典
The Worship Ceremony at the Yellow Emperor Mausoleum

Pic. 1　Dragon Dancing Performance Illustrated by Mathew Russel

黄帝陵是中华民族始祖轩辕黄帝的陵墓，位于陕西省延安

The Yellow Emperor[①] Mausoleum is the tomb of the Yellow Emperor (whose given name was Xuanyuan), the founding ancestor of

---

[①] A figure whose historicity is disputed. He was purportedly the son of Shaodian (少典) and his family name was Gongsun (公孙). He was said to live by the River Ji (姬水), and so he received another family name Ji (姬). But since he was born in a hill named Xuanyuan (轩辕), he was also named thereafter, and was even more often called Xuanyuan Huangdi (轩辕黄帝). Huangdi founded his kingdom in a place named Youxiong (有熊), thereby gaining Youxiong (有熊) as a further title. And most importantly, Huangdi, for his greatest merits and virtues, was embraced and supported by all the surrounding tribes as the paramount king. Since his kingdom in the central region of China took the yellow colour of the loess earth as an auspicious sign, the Yellow Emperor (黄帝) became his most popular name. For all these reasons, he is perpetually worshipped as the patriarch of the Chinese nation.

市黄陵县的桥山之上。这里除黄帝陵外，还有轩辕庙、祭祀大殿、祭亭、黄帝手植柏等。

轩辕黄帝开启了中华文明之先河，被奉为"人文始祖"。为了纪念和缅怀黄帝，在黄帝"驭龙升天"之后，先民就开展了隆重的祭祀活动。据《绎史》记载："黄帝崩，其臣左彻取衣冠几杖而庙祀之。"后世帝王祭祀黄帝，最早见诸史料的是周威烈王四年（前422）秦灵公作吴阳上畤，专祭黄帝。汉代以后，祭祀黄帝成为朝廷定例。

1911年，孙中山先生就任临时大总统，

Chinese nation. It is located at Mount Qiao (literally "Bridge Mountain") in Huangling County, Yan'an City, Shaanxi Province. In addition to the mausoleum, the features of the site include the Xuanyuan Temple, the Main Sacrifice Hall, the sacrificial pavilion, and the cypress planted by the Yellow Emperor himself.

It was the Yellow Emperor who initiated Chinese civilisation and is therefore honoured as "the patriarch of the Chinese race". Following "his legendary ride on a dragon up to the heaven", people in ancient times began to hold grand memorial ceremonies to commemorate him. According to the *Yi Shi*, "Zuo Che, one of the officials during the reign of the Yellow Emperor, gathered and deposited the Yellow Emperor's clothes and mace in a temple to be worshipped after his death." Historical records report that Duke Ling of the State of Qin, was the first monarch recorded to worship the Yellow Emperor. He did so in 422 BC at the "Upper Altar" on the south side of Mount Wu (in modern-day Baoji, Shaanxi Province), a sacrificial site he designated exclusively for that purpose. Revering the Yellow Emperor has been a royal rite ever since.

In 1911, when Sun Yat-sen became the acting president of the Republic of China

派专人赴黄陵祭祖。抗日战争时期,国共两党多次共祭黄帝,毛泽东主席亲自撰写祭文。

黄帝陵祭祀活动在长期的实践中形成了一定的规模和祀典礼仪,大致分为公(官)祭、民祭两种形式。

现在的清明公祭黄帝陵仪式庄严、肃穆。祭陵现场的布置是在祭亭上悬挂一横额,上书"某某年清明公祭轩辕黄帝典礼",一般用农历纪年。祭桌上摆放祭器、香烛、时鲜水果、面花馒头等。祭祀的仪程主要有奏古乐、跳古舞、献花篮花圈、行三鞠躬礼、主持人恭读祭文、鸣放鞭炮、绕陵一周、植纪念树等。

(1911—1949), officials were sent to Huangling County to pay reverence to their ancestor. During the Anti-Japanese War, members of the Kuomintang and the Communist Party of China jointly offered sacrifices to the Yellow Emperor several times. One of the memorial eulogies they recited was composed by Chairman Mao himself.

Years of reverential practices at the mausoleum helped to form a codified calendar of sacrificial rites, which can be roughly divided into two forms: officially-organised sacrifices and civilian-organised sacrifices.

In the present day, a solemn official sacrificial ceremony is held at Qingming Festival (5th April on the Lunar Calendar, otherwise known as "Tomb Sweeping Day"). The layout of the sacrificial site can be described thus: a banner hangs on the sacrifice pavilion, emblazoned with the words "×× (year) the Yellow Emperor Official Sacrificial Ceremony". The year on the banner is formulated according to the Lunar Calendar, being the combination of the Heavenly Stems and Earthly Branches. On the sacrificial table are placed sacrificial utensils, incense and candles, fresh fruit, steamed buns topped with flowers kneaded from dough, and other items. The

民间祭祀多在清明节前后和重阳节期间举行。民祭活动除保留了公祭活动的一些内容外,更突出了民间性,增加了鼓乐队、唢呐队、仪仗队、三牲队。

改革开放以来,黄帝陵祭祀越来越受到海内外华夏儿女的关注,祭祀规模日渐宏大,祭祀礼仪日渐隆

ritual of the memorial ceremony includes the playing of ancient music, the performance of ancient dances, the offering up baskets of flowers and wreaths, bowing down physically three times, the ceremonial host reading a funeral oration, the letting off of firecrackers, pacing one circuit around the mausoleum, and planting memorial trees.

Local memorial ceremonies usually fall around Qingming Festival and on the Double Ninth Festival (9th September on the Lunar Calendar). Aside from the enactment of certain official sacrificial rites, local memorial ceremonies tend to bear a stronger folk culture flavour. They typically feature drum bands, *suona* [①] ensembles, guards of honour, and oblations involving three types of animals (horses, cattle and rams).

Since the advent of the Reform and Opening-up, memorial ceremonies at the Yellow Emperor Mausoleum have attracted ever greater attention, both at home and abroad. The scale, grandeur and solemnity of the rites

---

① The *suona*, also called *laba* or *haidi*, is a Chinese double-reeded horn. The *suona* appeared in China around the 3rd century CE. It produces a distinctively loud and high-pitched sound, and is used frequently in Chinese traditional music ensembles, particularly those which perform outdoors.

重。祭祀黄帝已成为传承中华文明、凝聚华夏儿女、共谋祖国统一、开创美好生活的一项重大活动。黄帝陵祭典已列入第一批国家级非物质文化遗产名录。

have increased accordingly. The Worship of the Yellow Emperor has become an activity of crucial significance since it embodies the inherited legacy of Chinese civilisation and allows the progeny of the Chinese race to unite in the cause of national reunification and in the pursuit of a better life. The Worship Ceremony at the Yellow Emperor Mausoleum was listed among the first batch of the National Intangible Cultural Heritage.

1.2 宝鸡民间社火
The Folk *Shehuo* Performance in the Baoji Area

社火是由先民祭祀土神的社日和祭祀火神的迎神赛会活动逐渐演变而产生的一种民间巡游演艺活动。史料记载和学者研究认为，中国社火

The *Shehuo*[①] performances (pyrotechnic and acrobatic performances) evolved from the festivities which ancient ancestors performed to worship the God of the Earth and the God of Fire. They are a popular folk custom in which farmer actors perform various acrobatics while parading through streets. According to historical

---

① *Shehuo* is a spontaneous traditional festive occasion for songs and dances prevailing mainly in the countryside of Northern China. With a long history, these festive affairs are rooted in primitive sacrificial activities in which ancient people prayed for harvest and affluence with their songs and dances from *She* (社), originally meaning the God of Earth, and *Huo* (火), literally meaning fire which ancient people believed to have the magic power of driving away evil spirits.

Pic. 2　Equestrian *Shehuo* Illustrated by Mathew Russell

发源于西秦宝鸡。宝鸡社火在其发展的历史长河中,由起初的集民间音乐、舞蹈、诗歌、杂耍、锣鼓为一体的戏剧形式逐渐发展为有固定特型的造型形式。

宝鸡社火按表演时间可分为昼社火和夜社火。其表演形式有造型社火和表演社火两大类。造型社火

records and scholarly research, the origins of *Shehuo* can be traced all the way back to the Baoji area in the State of Western Qin during the era of the Sixteen Kingdoms in China (385-431). Through history, the Baoji *Shehuo* performances gradually developed and matured to assume a fixed style. This was after years of development on the basis of its initial theatrical forms integrating folk music, dancing, poetry, and acrobatics as well as gongs and drums.

According to the time of day in which a performance is enacted, the Baoji *Shehuo* can be divided into two varieties: daytime *Shehuo* and evening *Shehuo*. In terms of performance style, there are two categories. The first kind

有背社火、马社火、芯子社火、山社火、面具社火等，进行列队表演；表演社火有地台社火、高跷社火等，主要在场院进行表演。宝鸡社火由于扮演的大多是古装历史剧和古典名著中的特型人物，所以服装头帽和道具、枪棒把子全是以古戏装形式出现。社火游演时一般是探马在前，后面跟着社火会旗、火铳队、旗队、社火队，最后是锣鼓队。社火游演队伍气势宏大，锣鼓喧天，热闹非凡，具有很高的民俗价值和审美价值。

is a static figurative display with mythical figures in costumes walking along the streets, standing on high-raised frames or riding on horseback. The second kind is a dynamic performance with farmers or amateur actors singing and dancing in the parade. The static figurative type encompasses Carrying *Shehuo* (farmer performers carrying a steel frame or rig on which child actors apparently balance), Equestrian *Shehuo* Performance (farmer performers riding on the backs of horses), *Xinzi Shehuo* (child players standing suspended on frames or rigs fashioned from steel and known as *Xinzi*), Mountain *Shehuo* (child players balancing on steel frames fashioned to resemble mountains) and Masked *Shehuo* (farmer actors performing with masks on or their faces painted), with parade-like processions walking the streets. The dynamic performance contains *Ditai Shehuo* (farmer actors performing on the ground or stage) and Stilt *Shehuo* (performers walking on elongated artificial legs), etc. Such performances are mainly conducted in a yard or on platforms in open spaces. Baoji *Shehuo* performances feature characters mainly drawn from Chinese historical plays and classic literary masterpieces. Therefore, all the props worn and used by actors, including costumes, hats, stage properties, spears and cudgels, etc. emulate relevant ancient designs for these articles. During *Shehuo* processions, performers arrange themselves into different formations (performing teams). The first formation, which leads the whole procession, is called the *Tanma* (scout horse or reconnaissance cavalry). Behind it are four formations, namely the formation of flags of different performing teams, the blunderbuss formation (blunderbuss-like props mounted on tractors), the colourful flags formation, and the performing team formation. The last in the procession is the gong and drum formation. The performing troupes are grand and imposing in scale. They create a hilarious, boisterous and bustling atmosphere with the deafening sound of gongs and drums as well as drawing a huge crowd. The event is therefore endowed with great aesthetic value further to its interest as a specimen of folk culture.

改革开放以来，宝鸡民间社火艺术得到发扬光大，成为群众喜闻乐见的一项文化活动，并多次随国家民间艺术团体出访演出，受到国外观众

Since the Reform and Opening-up in 1978, the Baoji *Shehuo* Performance has been augmented and developed into a spectacular social activity that ordinary people love to attend. This has won for these farmer performers the opportunity to step out of the country, with professional national folk art performing

1 陕西省第一批非物质文化遗产名录中的民俗
The Folk Culture in the First Batch of the Intangible Cultural Heritage in Shaanxi Province

Pic. 3　Stilt *Shehuo* Illustrated by Mathew Russell

的喜爱和欢迎。2003年，宝鸡被陕西省文化厅命名为"民间社火艺术之乡"。宝鸡民间社火已列入第一批国家级非物质文化遗产名录。

troops, to bring the *Shehuo* performance to other nations. It therefore enjoys great popularity both at home and abroad. In 2003, Baoji was designated as "Home of the *Shehuo* Performance as a Folk Art" by the Shaanxi Provincial Department of Culture. The Baoji *Shehuo* Performance was listed among the first batch of the National Intangible Cultural Heritage.

1.3 药王山庙会
The Mount Yaowang Temple Fair

药王山位于陕西省铜川市耀州区城东，为隋唐时期伟大的医药学家孙思邈归隐之处。药王山庙会因纪念孙思邈忌辰而产生，以弘扬药王孙思邈的医德医风、发扬继承祖国传统中医药文化为宗旨。

孙思邈系陕西耀州人，是我国医药学创新发展的开拓者和一代宗师。大约在唐代后期，人们就开始在这里为孙思邈立祠。北宋时，药王山庙会已在青明宫举行。明嘉靖时，庙会规模开始变大，会期变长，经月余不绝。从清末至今，会期为农历二月初二至二月十一。

Located in the eastern part of Yaozhou District in Tongchuan City, Shaanxi Province, Mount Yaowang (literally "King of Medicine") is where Sun Simiao, the great medical pedagogue of the Sui and Tang Dynasties, sought seclusion. The Mount Yaowang Temple Fair is staged on the anniversary of Sun Simiao's death in order to commemorate his contribution to medical ethics and to continue to inherit and promote the legacy of Traditional Chinese Medicine he bequeathed.

Sun Simiao, a native of Yaozhou in Shaanxi Province, was a pioneer and great master in the development of Chinese medical science. A temple was erected for him at around the time of the late Tang Dynasty (618–907). In the Northern Song Dynasty (960–1127), the Mount Yaowang Temple Fair was first held in the Qingming Palace. During the Jiajing Period of the Ming Dynasty (1522–1566), the temple fairs swelled in size and expanded in duration, lasting for more than a month. Ever since the late Qing Dynasty (1636–1911), the date of temple fair has fallen between 2nd and 11th of the lunar February.

1 陕西省第一批非物质文化遗产名录中的民俗
The Folk Culture in the First Batch of the Intangible Cultural Heritage in Shaanxi Province

Pic. 4　Praying for Blessings Illustrated by Mathew Russell

药王山庙会期间，数以万计的群众由四面八方云集而来，山上香烟缭绕，钟磬齐鸣，鼓乐喧天，人声鼎沸。大殿内，人人虔诚叩首，个个恭敬上香，许下美好心愿，祈求长寿健康。此外，这里每天还有路畔灯、狮子灯、龙灯、花火、天明戏等文化活动，非常热闹。药王山庙会已列入第一批国家级非物质文化遗产名录。

During the temple fair, tens of thousands of people flock to Mount Yaowang. The mountain top is wreathed in incense smoke and there is the simultaneous pealing of bells, together with the deafening chiming of stones and beating of drums. Spectators are engulfed in an atmosphere of tumult and clamour. Within the main hall, people kowtow and burn incense piously. They make good wishes before statues of deities they worship, praying for longevity and health for people they love as well as for themselves. In addition, on every day of the temple fair, one can witness lively cultural spectacles, such as three-dimensional roadside lanterns, lion-shaped lanterns, dragon-shaped lanterns, flower fire (molten iron being splashed o nto the ground to generate sparks) and the dawn opera(arias being sung from dusk to dawn). The Mount Yaowang Temple Fair has been listed among the first batch of the National Intangible Cultural Heritage.

1.4 延川小程村原生态民俗文化
The Original Ecological Folk Culture of Xiaocheng Village in Yanchuan County

小程村属陕西省延安市延川县土岗乡碾畔行政村。小程村地处陕北黄土高原东部、秦晋黄河大峡谷西侧，人口少，交通闭塞，靠天吃水，是个无水无电的贫困村。

Xiaocheng Village falls under the administration of Nianpan ("millstone-side") Village, in Tugang Town, Yanchuan County, Yan'an City, Shaanxi Province. The landlocked village is situated in the eastern region of the Loess Plateau in Northern Shaanxi and on the western side of the Grand Canyon of the Yellow River between the traditional territories of Qin (Shaanxi Province) and Jin (Shanxi Province). The village possesses a tiny population, being inaccessible to transportation. The domestic water supply is at the mercy of the weather. The community is almost devoid of water and electricity.

延川小程村原生态民俗文化是在古老的黄河历史文化积淀

The original ecological folk culture of Xiaocheng Village in Yanchuan County was spawned over time by the historical conditions

和几千年来农耕自然经济的生产方式和文化土壤中孕育产生的文化形态。由于这里交通闭塞，几千年来形成的原生态文化得以保存至今，诸如原始宗教的辟邪招魂、祭神求雨、祭河神、祈福保平安、谢土神等祭祀礼仪和婚丧嫁娶、节日风俗等古老民俗。此外，还有传统剪纸、刺绣、面花、民歌等民间艺术也得到了原生态的传承。它们共同形成了一个完整的原生态民俗文化村。

小程村有着天然的乾坤湾黄河景观。相传人文始祖伏羲看到

of the Yellow River. It also reflects the modes of agricultural production practiced here over thousands of years and the culture associated with that agrarian economy. Many of its features remain well-preserved in the present day due to its landlocked geography. These include sacrificial rites evocative of primitive religion, namely the warding-off of evil spirits and invoking of departed spirits, the worshipping of deities for rain and for blessings of peace and well-being, and giving thanks to the God of the Earth. With the addition of popular customs for matrimony, funerals and other festivities, this ecological culture forms an integral cycle of rites. Moreover, the traditional folk arts of paper-cutting, embroidery, and dough sculpture (kneading dough figures to top steamed buns), folk songs, and so forth, have also been inherited in an original ecological form. All of the aforesaid aspects endow the village with a complete original folk culture.

Xiaocheng Village is blessed with the Qiankun Bay,① the most magnificent scenery of a curving line to be found throughout the

---

① This appears as a looping bend in the river, also somewhat like the form of the Greek character omega. Its Chinese name is taken from the characters for the "heaven" (*Qian*) and the "earth" (*Kun*).

此景后受到启发，创立了太极八卦图。小程村内还有古城遗址，遗址的石刻上刻有千年古窑，古窑口上还有胡人、石花图案。小程村的民间民俗文化积淀深厚，原始、古朴的唢呐、秧歌、民间剪纸、刺绣、布堆画等都十分珍贵。

延川小程村民俗文化已有2 000多年的传承历史，是一个独

whole course of the Yellow River. Legend has it that Fuxi, or Fu Hsi, the creator of the human race in China, took this scene as his inspiration for designing the configuration of the Eight Trigrams① in *Taiji*.② Within the village, there is the site of a historical settlement. Therein stands a stone sculpture bearing the inscription "millennium kiln". The bricks which compose the kiln entrance were engraved with pattern of non-Han figures and flowers by the non-Han nationalities and feature the likeness of flowers in stone. Xiaocheng Village has accumulated a profound civilian folk culture. Its primitive and rustic *suona* horn, *yangge*③ dancing, paper-cutting, embroidery, cloth patchwork crafts, and so on are of superlative value.

With a history of more than 2,000 years, the folk culture of Xiaocheng Village can be described as a unique original ecological cultural

---

① The Eight Trigrams are *Qian* (heaven), *Kun* (earth), *Li* (fire), *Dui* (marsh), *Kan* (water), *Zhen* (thunder), *Xun* (wind), and *Gen* (mountain).
② *Taiji* is an ancient Chinese philosophy concerning the natural world and is one of the central elements of traditional Chinese culture. The word *Taiji* itself refers to the "great primal beginning" of all that exists, and is often translated as the "Supreme Ultimate".
③ *Yangge* is a broad category of Chinese performance referring to a form of dance or stylised movement, singing or chanting, and role-playing with wide-ranging regional variations. It is very popular in Northern China and is one of the most representative form of folk arts.

特的原生态文化博物馆和研究陕北历史和民俗文化的"活化石"。延川小程村原生态民俗文化已列入陕西省第一批非物质文化遗产名录。

museum and a "living fossil" useful for studying the history and folk culture of northern Shaanxi. The Original Ecological Folk Culture of Xiaocheng Village in Yanchuan County was listed among the first batch of the Intangible Cultural Heritage in Shaanxi Province.

1.5 骊山女娲补天
Nüwa① Mends the Sky at Mount Li

陕西省西安市临潼区地处关中平原中部。骊山为秦岭支脉，位于临潼区南，东西绵延25公里。古代骊戎国曾在此养马，故名"骊山"（古时名"丽山"）。

Lintong District in Xi'an City is located in the middle of the Guanzhong Plain (literally "within the Passes"②). In its south stands Mount Li, part of the Qinling Mountain Range, stretching for 25 kilometres from east to west. This was where the ancient Lirong regime once raised horses, hence the name Mount Li (the character *li* is different from its ancient name in intonation, with the present version being in the rising tone as 骊, while the ancient one being in the descending tone as 丽).

---

①Nüwa is the mother goddess of Chinese mythology, the sister and wife of Fuxi, the emperor-god. She is credited with creating humanity and repairing the Pillar of Heaven.
②The Passes which enclose the Guanzhong Plain are as follows: the Tongguan Pass in the east, the Sanguan Pass in the west, the Wuguan Pass in the south and the Xiaoguan Pass in the North.

骊山女娲是华夏民族的始祖。传说女娲炼石补天后人类才得以安居，文明才得以延续。骊山女娲风俗经过千百年的传承和发展，逐步形成了形式多样的骊山女娲文化。

骊山女娲风俗主要有民间节日（如正月初七的人日、六月十五的老母会等）、民间习俗（如祭祀灶王爷、中秋拜月等）、民间婚丧嫁娶风俗，生子风俗等。骊山女娲风俗也体现在民间剪纸、刺绣、面塑作品

Nüwa is believed to have been the creator of the Chinese nation. Legend has it that it was only after Nüwa smelted rocks to repair the sky, perhaps here at Mount Li, that human beings were able to live in peace and that civilisation could be sustained. Thousands of years of heritage and development have meant that the customs associated with Nüwa have gradually evolved into a variegated Nüwa culture.

The customs of Nüwa at Mount Li mainly involve folk festivals (like Human's Day, on the 7th day of the lunar January, the Laomu[①] Fair on the 15th of the lunar June), folk customs (like offering sacrifices to the Kitchen God[②], worshipping the moon at Mid-Autumn Festival), rites associated with weddings and funerals, as well as postnatal customs. They are also embodied in crafts such as paper-cutting, embroidery and dough sculpture. The customs

---

① Laomu is a popular female immortal in the Taoist pantheon, and a high-ranking one according to some later sources. Her origins are said to derive from Nüwa, the legendary creator and mother goddess.

② The Kitchen God, also known as the God of the Hearth, is a popular deity most Chinese would worship every year on the "off year" (the 23rd day of the lunar December) with *niangao* offered as a sacrifice since he is believed to watch over the domestic affairs of a family. Chinese homes have a paper image or picture of the deity hung throughout the year near the family's hearth.

中。骊山女娲风俗是古代人类社会生活的"活化石"。它不但展现了中华民族文化创造力的杰出价值,而且对维系中华民族的文化传承具有重要意义。弘扬女娲文化对于淳化民风、提高民族凝聚力和加深民族感情也有着积极的作用。骊山女娲风俗已列入陕西省第一批非物质文化遗产名录。

of Nüwa at Mount Li are one of the "living fossils" which preserve the ancient social lives of human beings. They not only demonstrate the outstanding value of the cultural creativity of the Chinese nation, but also play an important role in maintaining the cultural inheritance of the Chinese nation. Safeguarding Nüwa culture helps to protect the pure essence of Chinese culture and can serve to strengthen national cohesion and enhance national sentiment. The Customs of Nüwa at Mount Li was listed among the first batch of the Intangible Cultural Heritage in Shaanxi Province.

1.6 长武道场
The Taoist Rite in Changwu County

长武道场俗称"打醮",清代中期起源于陕西省咸阳市长武县彭公乡方庄村,迄今已有200余年的历史,是一种融鼓器乐和说

The Taoist rite performed in Changwu Country, commonly known as *Dajiao*①, has a history stretching back more than 200 years. It dates back to the middle period of the Qing Dynasty and originates from Fangzhuang Village, Penggong Township, Changwu County,

---

① *Dajiao* is a Taoist ritual and festival which is performed to pray and request that the Taoist deities bestow peace and harmony in the particular neighbourhood or locale.

Pic. 5　The Taoist Rite in Changwu Illustrated by Mathew Russell

唱为一体的宗教祭祀性综合艺术形式，长期流传于陕、甘交界地区。

　　长武道场是一种集自然与幽灵、祭祀与民俗、道德与人性于一体的民间文化现象，借助于宗教、民俗、礼仪活动世代相传。长武道场的表演

Xianyang City, Shaanxi Province. The rite is a comprehensive art form, involving sacrificial religious activities being performed to the accompaniment of drum music and chanting. This type of ritual has long been prevalent in the borderlands between Shaanxi Province and Gansu Province.

　　The Taoist rite in Changwu is a folk cultural phenomenon, which combines apparently paradoxical elements, including nature and spirits, sacrifices and customs, morality and humanity. It has been passed down from generation to generation by virtue of religion, folk customs and ceremonies. The Taoist rite

者由 7~8 人组成，称"羽士"或"居士"，常身着黄、蓝、黑道袍，头戴道冠，列队表演。演奏乐器有小鼓、管子等 10 多种。演唱内容有《道经》《孝经》等。演奏形式多是行乐。曲牌有《赞八仙》《菩萨登台》等 30 多种。音乐韵调古朴低沉，悠扬委婉，有独特的感染力。

长武道场原为宗教活动，在长期的发展过程中，逐渐演变为世俗性的礼仪活动。除用于祭神祀鬼外，还

in Changwu is enacted by seven or eight Taoist priests called *yushi* or lay devotees called *jushi*,① wearing yellow, blue or black Taoist vestments and a Taoist mitre, forming a parade. More than 10 kinds of musical instruments, including snare drums and pipes, are played. *Tao Ching* (the first 37 chapter of *Tao Te Ching*) and the *Classic of Filial Piety* (*Xiao jing*②) are chanted in the procession accompanied by *xingyue* (walking music, with players standing or walking, while playing, instead of sitting). Over 30 typical tunes are always played, including *Commending the Eight Immortals* (*Zan ba xian*) and *Bodhisattva Ascending to the Stage* (*Pu sa deng tai*). They are unsophisticated and low-spirited but melodious in their musical rhythms, creating a distinct and appealing atmosphere.

The Taoist rite in Changwu was originally a religious activity by nature. However, over the longer term it gradually evolved into a ritual embracing more secular and lay features. In addition to offering sacrifices to deities and

---

① *Jushi* refers to a householder. Most broadly, it refers to any layperson, and most narrowly, to a wealthy and prestigious familial patriarch.
② The *Classic of Filial Piety* (*Xiao jing*) is a Confucian classic treatise giving advice on filial piety, that is to say, how to behave towards a senior such as a father, an elder brother, or a ruler.

用于民间殡葬、庆寿、庙会活动中，借以祛除灾祸、祈福纳祥、延年益寿，是道教遗留下来的一份较为完整和独特的民俗艺术遗产。长武道场已列入陕西省第一批非物质文化遗产名录。

ghosts, it has also come to embrace funerals, senior people's birthday celebrations, and temple fair activities in order to dispel disasters and pray for blessings, prosperity and longevity. Overall, the rite can be described as a relatively comprehensive and unique specimen of folk art heritage built on the basis of Taoism. It was listed among the first batch of the Intangible Cultural Heritage in Shaanxi Province.

1.7 炎帝陵祭典

The Worship Ceremony at the Mausoleum of the Yan Emperor

陕西省宝鸡市是炎帝故里。据民间传说，宝鸡地区的炎帝祭祀活动可追溯至黄帝时期。约在5000年前，炎帝因误尝火焰子（俗名"断肠草"）而逝于宝鸡天台山。黄帝闻听后，急速赶往天台山祭奠。秦灵公三年（前422），秦人开始祭祀炎帝、黄帝，开创了官方祭祀炎帝

Baoji City in Shaanxi Province was the hometown of the Yan Emperor or the Flame Emperor. According to folklore, the worship ceremony for Yan in the Baoji area can be traced back to the reign of the Yellow Emperor. About 5,000 years ago, Yan died in the vicinity of Mount Tiantai in Baoji as a result of his mistakenly ingesting the root of a herb called sungpan monkshood (also known as *huo yan zi*, and commonly called the "heartbroken herb"). Upon hearing the sad news, the Yellow Emperor hurried to Mount Tiantai to pay his respects. In 422 BC, people in the land of the

1 陕西省第一批非物质文化遗产名录中的民俗
The Folk Culture in the First Batch of the Intangible Cultural Heritage in Shaanxi Province

Pic. 6 The Yan Emperor Illustrated by Mathew Russell

的先例。

20世纪80年代初，祭祀炎帝活动开始在民间兴起。20世纪90年代初，在宝鸡市原河滨公园（现炎帝园）易地重修了炎帝祠，在常羊山重修了炎帝陵。自此，每年的清明节和炎帝忌日，都会在炎帝祠、炎帝陵举行规模宏大的祭祀典礼。祭祀程序包括全体肃立、鸣钟

Qin began to formally revere the Yan Emperor and the Yellow Emperor, initiating the official precedent of worshipping Yan Emperor.

The early 1980s witnessed the emergence of popular activities reverencing the Yan Emperor. The Ancestral Temple of the Yan Emperor was rebuilt in the early 1990s within the Riverside Park (present-day Yandi Park) in Baoji City. The Mausoleum of the Yan Emperor was rebuilt on Mount Changyang. Since then, large-scale worship ceremonies have been held in the Ancestral Temple of the Yan Emperor and the Mausoleum of the Yan Emperor every year on the day of Qingming Festival and on the memorial day of the Yan Emperor's death as well. The worship rituals include: worshippers

奏乐、敬献祭品、奠酒、敬献花篮、主祭人读祭文。仪式完毕后，全体肃立，向炎帝行礼。至此礼毕。

炎帝和黄帝同为中华民族的人文始祖，是中华文明的缔造者。宝鸡炎帝陵祭典活动以一种文化的典礼"追中华文化之根，缅先祖功业之德"，传播全球华人同根同祖的民族观念，这对于宣传民族文化，弘扬爱国主义情感，促进海峡两岸的统一及世界各地炎黄子孙的感情交流有着重要的影响和作用。炎帝陵祭典已列入第一批国家级非物质文化遗产名录。

standing still in reverence, bells being struck, the playing of ancient music, the offering of sacrifices and libation, the offering of baskets of flowers, and the chief acolyte reading the eulogy. After the aforesaid procedures are completed, all worshippers stand solemnly to salute the Yan Emperor.

Both the Yan Emperor and the Yellow Emperor were mortal forefathers of the Chinese nation and founders of Chinese civilisation. The worship activity at the Mausoleum of the Yan Emperor is a cultural ceremony that seeks out the root of Chinese culture and recalls the virtues of our ancestors. It enshrines the principle of the Chinese nation sharing a common root and a common ancestor and consequently plays an important role in publicising national culture and patriotism. It serves to further promote cross-strait unity between Mainland China and Taiwan and highlight the emotional bond shared between the descendants of the Yan Emperor and the Yellow Emperor all over the world. The Worship Ceremony at the Mausoleum of the Yan Emperor was listed among the first batch of the National Intangible Cultural Heritage.

1.8 司马迁民间祭祀
Venerating Sima Qian [①]

Pic. 7　The Sima Qian Temple Illustrated by Mathew Russell

陕西省韩城市嵬东乡（已并入芝川镇）徐村是我国伟大的文学家、史学家司马迁的故里和真骨墓所在地。这里也是司马迁后裔冯、同两姓族人的居住地。在这里"冯同一家""冯同不分"，

Situated within the territory of Weidong Town (present-day Zhichuan Town) in Hancheng City, Shaanxi Province, Xu Village is the hometown and the burial site of Sima Qian, the ancient Chinese litterateur and historian. It is also where his descendants, with the family names Feng and Tong, continue to make their home. In this village people who share these two family names are like one giant clan, with

---

[①] He is considered the father of Chinese historiography for his *Records of the Grand Historian* (*Shi ji*), a general history of China covering more than 2,000 years beginning from the rise of the legendary Yellow Emperor and the formation of the first Chinese polity to the reign of the Emperor Wu of the Han Dynasty.

两姓共进一个祠堂，共祭一个祖先，共称司马迁为"司马爷"。

司马迁民间祭祀是徐村特有的一种祭祖活动，自西汉形成以来，迄今已有2000多年的历史。每年清明节前夕午夜时分，冯、同两姓族人由长者率领，着礼服，抬香案、供品，在司马迁墓旁敬神祭祖。

与此同时，在墓旁

no distinction among its members. They worship their common ancestor at the same ancestral temple, all of them addressing Sima Qian as "Grandpa Sima".

The veneration of Sima Qian is an activity unique to Xu Village, having been practiced for more than 2,000 years ever since the establishment of the community in the Western Han Dynasty (206 BC－25 CE). On the eve of Qingming Festival every year, led by their elders, the Feng and Tong families, wear formal costumes and carry incense tables and offerings to worship the deities and their ancestors alongside Sima Qian's tomb.

Meanwhile, a makeshift stage is erected

Pic. 8　Stage-running Illustrated by Mathew Russell

搭台唱戏。黎明时分突然戏台上灯火全灭,鼓乐皆停。演员不卸妆,乐人携乐器,均从台上跑下。早有准备的村民立即拆舞台,抬香案,跟在演员后面向村东九郎庙狂奔,履失不准找,冠掉不能拾。演员和乐人跑到九郎庙戏台子上,大戏又接着开演。这就是当地群众所说的"跑台子戏"。

清明这一天,徐村街道竖起用松柏枝搭成的脚楼,家家彩灯高悬,门口贴着大红对联,村中小商小贩云集,亲戚朋友纷至沓来,比过年还要喜庆热闹。

徐村祭祀先祖司马迁的习俗在中国大地上绝无仅有,具有

by the tomb side for the performance of local opera. At dawn, the stage lights are extinguished and the drums and music cease abruptly. Actors run down from the stage without removing their makeup, and so do the musicians still carrying their instruments. Well-prepared villagers immediately begin to dismantle the stage and carry incense tables to run wildly after the actors to the Jiulang Temple in the east of the village. People run so fast that they have no time to stop and pick up their hats or shoes when they drop off while in motion. The performance resumes the moment when the actors and musicians mount the stage in the Jiulang Temple. This is what local people call the "stage-running opera".

On the day of Qingming Festival, turrets fashioned from pine and cypress branches are erected on the streets in Xu Village. Colourful lanterns are hung high up on the gates of houses, with red couplets on the two sides of doorframes. Vendors are attracted to the village, with friends and relatives visiting one after another. The festive atmosphere of the village is more conspicuous than that of Spring Festival.

The ancestral worship of Sima Qian in Xu Village is unique in China and has huge historical and cultural value. The Popular Worship of Sima

很高的历史和文化价值。司马迁民间祭祀已列入陕西省第一批非物质文化遗产名录。

Qian was listed among the first batch of the Intangible Cultural Heritage in Shaanxi Province.

1.9 东庄神楼
The Deity Tower in Dongzhuang Village

陕西省韩城市西庄镇东庄村的抬神楼被誉为"社火之王",是社火队伍中最受人们欢迎的一种民间舞蹈形式,也是全国社火表演艺术中独一无二的一枝奇葩。

Carrying the *Shenlou* (Deity Tower) is honoured as the "King of *Shehuo* performance", the most popular of its kind in Dongzhuang Village, Xizhuang Town, Hancheng City, Shaanxi Province. It is also a unique version of this art form among *Shehuo* performances nationwide.

Pic. 9　Carrying the *Shenlou* (Deity Tower) Illustrated by Mathew Russell

神楼是祭祀活动中用于抬神像的轿子，不同的祭祀活动所抬神灵不同。广泛分布于韩城各乡镇的祈雨神楼中的神灵是龙王。西庄镇有一座元代修建的法王庙，东庄神楼中所抬的神灵就是庙中所祭祀的法王房寅。房寅是韩城历史上的名医，后被封为法王。每年清明节，西庄镇的群众都要送法王归庙，火铳开道、锣鼓伴奏，十六台法王神楼被千百人拥着赫然出现。一旦锣鼓队敲起震天动地的祭祀锣鼓，开道的武神楼便左冲右突，如脱缰之马，神楼上的铜铃声扣人心弦，人们的呐喊声震谷裂川。在韩城的社火表演活动中，东庄法王神楼表演最为威武雄壮，遐迩闻名。

The Deity Tower is in fact the sedan chair used to carry statues of gods in a worship ceremony. The deities borne may vary according to which sacrificial rite is being enacted. The Dragon King is always to be found sitting in the petitioning-for-rain *Shenlou* in the villages and towns of Hancheng. In Xizhuang Town, there stands the Fawang (King of Law) Temple built in the Yuan Dynasty (1271–1368). The deity sitting in the Dongzhuang Deity Tower is named Fang Yin, King of Law, who is worshipped in the Fawang Temple. Fang Yin was a renowned doctor in ancient Hancheng, who was later appointed as King of Law. On each day of Qingming Festival, villagers in Xizhuang Town will escort the Fawang back to the temple dedicated to him. At the vanguard of the parade are vehicles bearing blunderbusses. To the accompaniment of gongs and drums, 16 Deity Towers with seated Fawang appear dramatically on the street, in front of an audience of tens of thousands. The *Wu Shenlou* (Martial Deity Tower) begins its performance by rushing forwards fiercely like a rampant horse the moment the gongs and drums play. The bronze bells hanging on the tower ring in a thrilling manner as people cheer on at deafening volume. In this way, the *Fawang Shenlou* performance has become the superlative acrobatic performance of this nature in Hancheng, its magnificence being well-known far and wide.

东庄神楼（包括韩城其他抬神楼）是迄今为止国内仅存的一种舞神楼形式，因而加强抢救和保护工作显得重要而有意义。东庄神楼已列入陕西省第一批非物质文化遗产名录。

The Dongzhuang Deity Tower (together with other Deity Tower Carrying Rituals in Hancheng City) is so far the last of its kind still extant in China. Conserving and supporting the custom therefore should be enhanced as a matter of great importance and significance. The Dongzhuang Deity Tower Carrying Rituals has been listed among the first batch of the Intangible Cultural Heritage in Shaanxi Province.

1.10 尧山圣母庙会
The Holy Mother Temple Fair at Mount Yao

尧山圣母庙建于陕西省渭南市蒲城县城北边的一座石质孤山上。庙中供奉的灵应夫人是以求雨、求子灵验而历代香火不断的女神。唐长庆二年（822），在山腰为诰封灵应夫人扩建了颇具规模的祠庙。宋崇宁年间，民间正式成立了尧山神社总社和

The Holy Mother Temple at Yaoshan (Mount Yao) was built on a rocky mountain in northern Pucheng County, Weinan City, Shaanxi Province. Enshrined within the temple is the goddess Madam Lingying (literally "efficacious"), who has been revered from generation to generation, for she is believed to be able to answer worshippers' petitions for rain or children. In 822 CE during the second year of the reign of the Emperor Muzong (795–824) of the Tang Dynasty, a full-sized temple was built on the mountainside for this goddess, whose title was

十一个分社。

每年清明期间,当地群众都要举行规模盛大的圣母庙会。蒲城及其周边地区数十万群众云集祠庙,举行烧香求子、求雨、神社迎神、送神、游神等传统祭祀活动。祭祀活动的准备工作从前一年农历八月十五就开始了,各村在此时也开始排练社火。在庙会中进行的社火游演以及扎纸花、演社戏、绕山、斗旗、表演尧山大鼓等活动都具有鲜明的地方特色。一千多年来,传统的祭祀礼仪活动被原汁原味地保留了下来,成为一个弥足珍贵的古文化载体,具有较高

imperially granted as Madam Lingying. During the Chongning regnal period (1102–1106) of the Emperor Huizong of Song, a general shrine as well as its eleven branches were established by ordinary people, with the centre being at Mount Yao.

During Qingming Festival, local people hold a grand Holy Mother Temple Fair. Hundreds of thousands of spectators from Pucheng County and its surrounding areas gather in the temple, burning incense to petition for children or rain and attending traditional deity-worshipping activities. The preparations for the worship activities commence a year earlier in the month of August on the fifteenth day according to the Lunar Calendar. Villagers begin to practise the *Shehuo* performances. Each temple fair features *Shehuo* as well as activities including making paper flowers, the performance of village operas, walking around the mountain and flag-fighting, and playing Mount Yao drums. The original form of the traditional worship activities has been preserved for over a thousand years. This makes it a precious repository for ancient culture, enjoying immense historical, artistic and academic value. The Holy Mother Temple Fair at Mount Yao was listed among the first batch of the Intangible

的历史价值、艺术价值和学术研究价值。尧山圣母庙会已列入陕西省第一批非物质文化遗产名录。

Cultural Heritage in Shaanxi Province.

1.11 蒲城血故事特技
The Pucheng Bloody Dumb Show

陕西省渭南市蒲城县的血故事特技源于上古先民镇妖驱邪的血祭风俗。每年正月十五、正月二十三和农历二月二，当地民间都以血故事特技的表演形式祛秽免灾，祈求神灵保佑五福临门、五谷丰登。

蒲城血故事是民间颂扬除暴安良、侠肝义胆、扶正祛邪、反腐倡廉等朴素正义理念的载体。血故事特技是以民间传说、历史事件为内容的"血刃、血耻"故事造型，以"惊、险、奇"著

The Pucheng Bloody Dumb Show as performed in Pucheng County, Weinan City, Shaanxi Province, has its origins in the ancient custom of resorting to blood sacrifice as a means of suppressing evil and driving out demons. Every 15th January, 23rd January and 2nd February according to the Lunar Calendar, local people put on a gory stunt-filled display in the hope of vanquishing evil and disaster and petitioning the gods for blessings and bountiful harvests.

The Pucheng Bloody Dumb Show upholds the crude logic of banishing the cruel and pacifying the bad, and of supporting the righteous and expelling the evil. On another level it shows how corruption ought to be curbed and integrity advocated, among other things. Based on stories and historical events concerning "the bloody blade" (killing evil) and "bloody shame" (exacting revenge), the scenarios

1 陕西省第一批非物质文化遗产名录中的民俗
The Folk Culture in the First Batch of the Intangible Cultural Heritage in Shaanxi Province

称。在表演过程中,老艺人提前设好机关,在车上或马上的表演者经过几个回合的武打后,随即出现分身、换掉人头等造型。血故事表演的突出特点是真人真械,鲜血淋漓,令人怵目惊心。表演前,血故事社火会要举行隆重的祭祀活动。蒲城自清代起开始创立血故事社火会,并立有严格的会规、会训。血故事社火会一直传承至今,现任会长雷德运是血故事社火会第十八代传人。

蒲城血故事特技是独具特色的非物质文化遗产,具有很高的观赏价值、历史价值和学术研究价值。蒲城血故事特技已列入陕西省第一批非物质文化遗产名录。

consist of stunts which appear shocking, dangerous and remarkable. In preparation for the performance, experienced artists set up concealed devices. These help the actors mounted on tractors or horses to engage in several rounds of acrobatic combat before using prosthetics to create the illusion of disembowelment and decapitation. The players and weapons in the bloody dumb show are both real, with knives, long spears or cleavers being plentiful. The spectacle is apparently gore-drenched and shocking. Before the performance, the associated *Shehuo* troupe will hold a grand worship ceremony. The Pucheng Bloody Dumb Show Society was established in the Qing Dynasty (1636–1911), with its own strict rules and disciplines and has been passed down from generation to generation up until today. The incumbent head of the society is Lei Deyun, the 18th holder of that post.

The Pucheng Bloody Dumb Show is an unique intangible cultural heritage, greatly cherished and possessing high historical and academic value. The Pucheng Bloody Dumb Show was listed among the first batch of the Intangible Cultural Heritage in Shaanxi Province.

1.12 谷雨祭祀文祖仓颉典礼

Grain-Rain Day Veneration of Cang Jie, the Inventor of Chinese Characters

陕西省渭南市白水县自古就有清明祭黄帝、谷雨祭仓颉的民间习俗。

仓颉是黄帝时期的史官，是中华象形文字的创始人，世代尊其为文字初祖。相传，仓颉创造了文字，结束了结绳记事。此事感动了天帝，天帝便向人间下了一场谷雨。这就是我国二十四节气中谷雨节的来历，也是后人在谷雨祭祀仓颉的缘由。

谷雨祭祀仓颉是

Since ancient times, Baishui County in Weinan City, Shaanxi Province, has held its own folk customs for reverencing the Yellow Emperor during Qingming Festival and Cang Jie on Grain-Rain Day.

Cang Jie is thought to have once been an official historian and record keeper during the reign of the Yellow Emperor (about 2,500 BC). He is credited with inventing pictographic characters. He was honoured by generations as the initiator of Chinese script. Legend has it that his invention put to an end the practice of recording events through tying knots in rope. This innovation touched the God of Heaven, who bestowed the earth with a grain-nourishing downpour. This is the origin of the Grain-Rain, the sixth of the 24 *Jieqi* [①] on the traditional Chinese Lunar Calendar. It also explains why people pay homage to Cang Jie on this particular day.

This worship embodies the high value the

[①] *Jieqi*, known as Solar Terms, are days marking one of the 24 time buckets of the solar year on the traditional Chinese lunar calendar, and were used to indicate the alternation of seasons and climate changes in ancient China.

1 陕西省第一批非物质文化遗产名录中的民俗
The Folk Culture in the First Batch of the Intangible Cultural Heritage in Shaanxi Province

中华民族汉字情结的具体表现。白水县建有仓颉庙,每年谷雨时节的仓颉庙会,场面隆重热烈,世代沿袭,约定成俗。近年来,祭祀仓颉活动的规模更大,参与者更广,全国文化名流和海外侨胞纷至沓来,谒祖祭圣。通过近年来的谷雨祭祀仓颉活动,逐渐形成了以仓颉文化为主导的区域特色文化,推动了渭北以古文化为主题的旅游事业,促进了区域社会经济的快速发展。

汉字的诞生是华夏文明的主要标志之一,而仓颉这位文化之神则是华夏文明的重要象征。保护和传承谷雨祭祀仓颉礼仪,

Chinese nation attaches to its alphabet. There is a Cang Jie Temple in Baishui County (the name can be literally translated as "White Water County"). The temple fairs held every year on Grain-Rain Day constitute a grand and lively spectacle and the worship tradition has been inherited by generation after generation until now. In recent years, worship activities have taken place on a greater scale with more participants. National cultural celebrities and even overseas Chinese come to pay homage to their ancestors and the sages. In recent years, the worship activities on Grain-Rain Day have helped to form a regionally-distinctive culture centred on Cang Jie. This has served to promote tourism on the theme of ancient culture in the area to the north of the River Wei.① As a result, the social economy of the region has enjoyed a massive boost.

The birth of Chinese characters is one of the key advents in the genesis of Chinese civilisation. Meanwhile, Cang Jie, the god of culture, is an important representative of Chinese civilisation. Seen in this light, the protection and inheritance of the rituals of worshipping Cang

---

① The River Wei is a major river in west-central China's Gansu and Shaanxi provinces. It is the largest tributary of the Yellow River and very important in the early development of Chinese civilisation.

就是保护中华民族传统文化，其历史文化价值重大，意义深远。谷雨祭祀文祖仓颉典礼已列入陕西省第一批非物质文化遗产名录。

Jie on Grain-Rain Day helps to preserve the traditional culture of the Chinese nation. Hence, it is of great value and far-reaching significance, both historically and culturally. The Grain-Rain Day Veneration of Cang Jie, the inventor of Chinese characters, was listed among the first batch of the Intangible Cultural Heritage in Shaanxi Province.

1.13 白云山庙会
The Mount Baiyun Temple Fair

白云山地处陕西省榆林市佳县城南的崇山峻岭中，因山上建有道教名胜白云观而得名，是全国著名的道教名山和风景区。山上的白云观是西北地区最大的明清古建筑群。白云观供奉的神以真武大帝与道教系列神为主，儒、释、道三教交汇。白云山

Located in the uplands of southern Jiaxian County in Yulin City, Shaanxi Province, Mount Baiyun, also known as the White Cloud Mountain, is a famous national Taoist mountain and scenic spot, named after a well-known Taoist site—the Baiyun Temple—which is to be found there. The Baiyun Temple is the largest ancient complex built in the Ming (1368–1644) and Qing Dynasties (1636–1912) in northwestern China. The principal deities worshipped within the Baiyun Temple are the Great Emperor of the Perfect Martiality[①] (*Zhen wu da di*) and other

---

[①] Also called Xuantian Shangdi (玄天上帝) (High Emperor of the Mysterious Heaven), or Xuanwu (玄武) (Mysterious or Black Warrior). In popular religion he is the deity representing the cardinal direction of north, and one of the highest deities in the Taoist pantheon.

庙会已有400多年的历史，是集宗教、文化、文物、艺术、旅游等于一体的古老而传统的集会。

白云山每年农历三月三、四月八和九月九举行传统庙会，其中尤以四月八庙会最为盛大。庙会期间有丰富多彩的迎贡、放赦、行香等道士科仪活动和许愿、酬神等信士活动，内容丰富，

Taoist deities, together with the saints of Confucianism and ancient Indian Buddhism. Enjoying a history of more than 400 years, the Mount Baiyun Temple Fair is an ancient and traditional gathering that integrates religion, culture, cultural relics, art and tourism.

Traditional temple fairs are held on Mount Baiyun every year on 3rd March, 8th April and 9th September according to the Lunar Calendar. Among these, the temple fair on 8th April on the lunar calendar is the grandest. The temple fairs here witness a variety of activities superintended by Taoist priests, like receiving tributes, sliding deities down from the top of the cliff, offering incense, and so on. Taoist believers are also

Pic. 10 Sliding Deities down from the Cliffs Illustrated by Mathew Russell

形式多样，充满了神秘的宗教气氛。白云山庙会规模宏大，山西、内蒙古、宁夏、甘肃等地群众也纷纷前来参加，场面极为壮观。

seen to make vows, and give thanks to the immortals. All of those activities contribute to the mysterious and spiritual atmosphere of the fair. With their grand scale and spectacular scenes, the temple fairs on Mount Baiyun attract plenty of people from nearby Shanxi Province, the Inner Mongolia Autonomous Region, the Ningxia Hui Autonomous Region, Gansu Province, and other places.

白云山道教属全真道龙门派。它在继承发展中国土生土长的传统道教的同时，又兼容了陕北黄土文化、黄河文化和大漠草原文化，形成了独具地方特色的白云山庙会文化。白云山庙会承载着陕北黄土高原上许多重大的历史文化信息和原始记忆，具有很高的历史价值、

Mount Baiyun Taoism can be categorised as belonging to the Longmen Lineage, one of the branches of Quanzhen Taoism[①] (known as Completion of Authenticity, or Complete Reality, or Complete Perfection). Built on the foundation of traditional Chinese Taoism, Mount Baiyun Taoism represents the fusion of the loess culture of northern Shaanxi Province, the Yellow River culture, and the culture of the desert and prairie. The end result is a local temple fair boasting a unique regional flavour. Enshrining vital historical and cultural information and preserving primitive memories of the Loess

---

① Currently the dominant branch of Taoism in continental China. It originated in Northern China in 1170 under the Jin Dynasty (1115−1234). One of its founders was the Taoist Wang Chongyang. When the Mongols invaded the Song Dynasty (960−1279) in 1254, the Quanzhen Taoists led by the Seven Masters of Quanzhen (全真七子) exerted great effort in keeping the peace, thus saving thousands of lives, particularly among those of Han Chinese descent.

文化价值、学术价值和旅游价值。白云山庙会已列入陕西省第一批非物质文化遗产名录。

Plateau in northern Shaanxi, the Mount Baiyun Temple Fair is of great historical, cultural, academic and tourist value. The Mount Baiyun Temple Fair was listed among the first batch of the Intangible Cultural Heritage in Shaanxi Province.

1.14 洋县悬台社火艺术

The *Shehuo* Performance on Suspended Stages in Yang County

陕西省汉中市洋县悬台社火又称洋县高芯子社火。此种社火以古装戏剧角色站在高台梁架上为表演形式。它汇集了民间各种社火的精华，为陕西南部的洋县城乡所特有。

洋县悬台社火迄今已有300多年历史。它源于商周时期，清代雍正时从众多的社火品种中脱颖而出，成为洋县社火中最有影

The *Shehuo* Performance on Suspended Stages in Yang County, Hanzhong City, Shaanxi Province, is also known as the *Shehuo* Performance on High *Xinzi* (frames made from steel). This features child players from the villages dressed in costumes like the characters from Shaanxi Opera and standing on steel *Xinzi* frames. This represents a fusion of the essence of various performances of this genre and is unique to the towns and villages of Yang County in southern Shaanxi Province.

The *Shehuo* Performance on Suspended Stages in Yang County enjoys a history of more than 300 years. Originating from the Shang (1600 BC–1046 BC) and Zhou (1046 BC–256 BC) Dynasties, it outshone other performances of its kind in Yang County and became

响力的一种表演形式，一直延续至今。

洋县悬台社火有五六层梁架，高达12米左右，梁架上固定着由七八岁到十二三岁的儿童扮演的神话故事、民间故事、历史故事、戏曲故事中的人物，其装扮均为古戏装形式，营造出一种高悬、惊险、奇绝的艺术效果，给人以极大的视觉冲击力。高耸的芯子固定在汽车或拖拉机上，可以游巷串街，进行巡演。

洋县悬台社火原生态印记明显，是研究当地乃至中国戏剧、舞蹈、音乐、美术及杂技发展历史的"活化石"。洋县悬台社火艺术已列入第一批国家级非物质文化遗产名录。

established as the most influential style during the reign of the Emperor Yongzheng of Qing (1722—1735). The *Shehuo* Performance on Suspended Stages exerts considerable force even to this day.

The performance involves a rig of 5-6 levels of steel frames, extending to a height of about 12 metres. Children between the ages of 7 or 8 to 12 or 13 are bound and fastened to the vertical pillars on different levels of the frame. They are dressed in ancient costumes, evoking roles in fairytales, folk stories, historical stories, and operas. Aesthetically, the performance creates the impression of precariousness, being thrilling and extraordinary. The impact it delivers upon audiences is huge. Fixed atop cars or tractors, the towering steel *Xinzi* frames can be transported in a procession through the lanes and streets.

The *Shehuo* Performance on Suspended Stages in Yang County, has a unique pedigree, distinguishing it as a "living fossil", valuable for studying the developmental history of local, and even national, opera, dances, music, arts and acrobatics. The *Shehuo* Performance on Suspended Stages in Yang County was listed among the first b atch of the National Intangible Cultural Heritage.

1.15 安康市汉滨区龙舟风俗

Dragon Boat Racing in Hanbin District, Ankang City

Pic. 11　Dragon Boat Racing Illustrated by Mathew Russell

龙舟竞渡是流传于陕西省安康市的一种民俗活动，长期盛行于汉水之滨的安康市汉滨区各村镇。相传龙舟竞渡是为了纪念爱国诗人屈原而逐渐形成的。安康市汉

Dragon boat racing, a folk activity, has long been prevalent in villages and towns of Hanbin District in Ankang City, Shaanxi Province. Legend has it that dragon boat racing was invented in commemoration of the patriotic poet Qu Yuan.[①] The Dragon Boat Racing staged at Hanbin District in Ankang City has been a popular aquatic sport since the time of the

---

[①] Qu Yuan (340 BC−278 BC) is generally recognised as the first great Chinese poet. He initiated the style of *Sao*, which is named after his work *Li Sao*, in which he abandoned the classic four-character verses used in poems of the *Book of Songs*, and adopted verses with varying lengths, giving the poem a more flowing rhythm and greater latitude of expression.

滨区龙舟竞渡自北宋起成为民间水上竞技游乐活动，至明代已颇具规模，清代中期上升为官府活动。现在每年端午节，汉滨区各村镇都要派出龙舟参加竞渡比赛，场面宏大壮观，气氛紧张热烈。

龙舟竞渡作为一种民间习俗，集祭祀、祈福、竞技、斗志于一体，有集资、祭龙舟、下水仪式、竞赛、划对头、赢输笑一套程序化的比赛方法。比赛时，"汉水上龙舟数艘，每舟载二三十人，挥旗击鼓，木桨齐划，状如矢飞。上下竞渡，喝彩之声不绝"。

Northern Song Dynasty (960–1127). It grew to a considerable scale in the Ming Dynasty, and was promoted as an official activity in the mid-Qing Dynasty. In modern times, on every Dragon Boat Festival, each village and town in Hanbin District sends dragon boats to participate in the race. The ensuing scene is grand and spectacular and the atmosphere tense and enthusiastic.

As a folk custom, dragon boat racing combines in the functions of sacrificial ceremony, praying for blessings, competitive sport, and promoting team morale. A set series of procedures need to be followed, namely raising funds (begun many days in advance of the competition), offering sacrifices to the dragon boats, and rituals for launching the vessels. Some competitions require that each boat designate a competitor boat that it aims to beat. If the said crew does not succeed, its oarsmen must sing songs, kowtow or make a bow with their hands folded in front of them to the rival oarsmen, before challenging them to compete in the subsequent year. "During the race, several dragon boats are launched on the River Hanjiang, each loaded with twenty to thirty oarsmen. Guided by flags and goaded on by gongs and drums, dragon boats surge ahead

现在龙舟风俗已成为安康民俗文化的亮点和旅游文化的一张名片。安康市汉滨区龙舟风俗已列入陕西省第一批非物质文化遗产名录。

on the concerted force of their determined sculling. Throughout the race, cheers rise and fall in rhythm with the paddles."

Nowadays, the dragon boat race has become a highlight of folk culture and a calling card for the tourist industry in Ankang City and was listed among the first batch of the Intangible Cultural Heritage in Shaanxi Province.

1.16 延安老醮会
Ancient Sacrificial Rituals in Yan'an

延安的平安老醮九大会（简称老醮会）原是当地民众在民国十八年（1929）发生的重大灾难面前为稳定人心，以追念、祭奠因瘟疫而死去的"三代亡灵"为契机，以陕北源远流长的民间宗教信仰为纽带，以"祈保（人畜）平安"

The Ancient Sacrificial Rituals for Ensuring Safety held in turn by nine chapters in Yan'an (known as *Lao jiao hui*—Ancient Sacrificial Ceremony) was initially a religious activity. It was first held in the 18th year of the Republic of China era (1929) in order to provide solace for the local people and commemorate "three generations of the dead" (some estimates put this at 300,000 individuals) who perished in an epidemic that swept across the Loess Plateau[①] area. The ceremony is connected with long-

---

① The Loess Plateau is enormously important to Chinese history, as it formed one of the early cradles of Chinese civilisation. Its eroded silt is responsible for the great fertility of the North China Plain, along with the repeated and massively destructive floods of the Yellow River.

为主题，集成舞蹈、音乐、戏曲等多种文化形式，形成的黄土地上一个综合性的大型文化活动。

standing northern Shaanxi folk beliefs and is centred on the purpose of "praying for safety for human beings and livestock". In the present day, the ceremony takes the form of a comprehensive grand cultural activity that integrates various practices including dancing, music and opera.

Pic. 12　Dropping Streamers Illustrated by Mathew Russell

延安老醮会"祈保（人畜）平安"这一主题思想，通过村民动手制作和张挂"平安吊"彩笺，扎制和装置纸佛塔，通过诵经、献祭、礼拜等公众仪式，更通过唱阳歌、打

The theme of "praying for safety for human beings and livestock" is not only vividly expressed through the villagers making and hanging colourful paper cuttings, called *ping' an diao* and crafting paper pagodas in public, but also demonstrated through the chanting of scriptures, the offering of sacrifices, worship rituals and so forth. It is further manifested through elaborate

腰鼓、转九曲等具有浓厚艺术色彩的主体行为得到多方面的突出表现。延安老醮会活动的核心环节是升幡、扬幡和收幡，目的是追悼"三代亡灵"。其活动形式古老、深奥而又美观。

延安老醮会具有凝聚民心、鼓励民众不屈抗争、维系社会秩序安定等积极的社会价值和文化价值。当前我国社会处于全面转型时期，保护延安老醮会并认真思考它如何在新的社会环境中获取新的生命空间，对于我们整个民族的精神生活取向有着积极的参照意义。延安老醮会已列入陕西省第一批非物质文化遗产名录。

special activities with strong local characteristics, like singing folk songs, playing waist drums and organizing the Jiuqu Yellow River Lantern Array activities. The principal rituals entail the sequence of raising streamers, waving streamers, and dropping streamers. That is to say that residents follow a local band heading out, marching back and forth in circular and spiral configurations, forming a parade, but all in a solemn fashion. The entire procedure is archaic in format, esoteric in content and graceful in sentiment.

The Ancient Sacrificial Rituals in Yan'an can be seen to exert a positive social and cultural influence. It unites and encourages people to stand firm against perceived evil while helping to foment social order. At present, China is experiencing a period of comprehensive transformation. Preserving the ceremony and actively trying to feel how it can be rejuvenated and reinvigorated within a new societal situation are of great significance. This can prove a point of positive reference for how the entire nation can orient itself spiritually. The Ancient Sacrificial Rituals in Yan'an was listed among the first batch of the Intangible Cultural Heritage in Shaanxi Province.

1.17 长安王曲城隍庙祭祀和庙会

The City God Temple Sacrificial Ceremony and Temple Fair at Wangqu Street in Chang'an District

陕西省西安市长安区王曲城隍庙所供奉的是汉高祖刘邦麾下大将纪信，当地民众每年都要举行大规模的祭祀活动。西汉文景二帝时，供奉的纪信由地皇神变为城隍神，不但继续掌管阴曹地府，还成为西汉长安城的保护神，并被后世皇帝封为总城隍，接受各地民众的祭祀。

王曲城隍庙祭祀在总城隍庙进行。总城隍庙建筑规模宏大，古雅壮观，可容纳数千人祭拜。除平常的祭祀活动外，每年农历二月初八纪信诞辰

The City God Temple in Chang'an District, Xi'an City, Shaanxi Province was built to revere Ji Xin, who served as a general under Liu Bang, otherwise known as the Emperor Gaozu of the Han Dynasty. Local people hold grand sacrificial ceremonies in the temple every year. During the reigns of the Emperors Wen and Jing of the Western Han Dynasty (202 BC−8 CE), Ji Xin, the God of the Land was promoted to be the God of City. He not only continued to preside over the netherworld as before, but also become the protector of Chang'an City in the Western Han Dynasty. Later, he was appointed by subsequent emperors as City God General and worshipped by people nationwide.

The sacrificial ceremonies of Wangqu City God Temple are held at the City God Temple General, which is storied and spectacular, and large enough to accommodate thousands of people. In addition to the routine ritual activities, the City God Temple General in Wangqu also welcomes people from around the country who

日，各地民众纷纷来到王曲总城隍庙祭祀纪信，以求得城隍爷的庇佑。由于祭祀活动规模宏大，逐渐形成庙会。庙会上有大戏、杂耍、锣鼓、社火、武术等民间艺术表演，受到广大民众的欢迎。长安王曲城隍庙祭祀和庙会已列入陕西省第一批非物质文化遗产名录。

come on the lunar 8th January, the anniversary of Ji Xin's birth, to pray for his blessings. As it grew larger and larger in scale, the sacrificial ceremony gradually evolved into a temple fair in which folk art performances, including traditional Chinese operas, juggling, gong and drum performances, *Shehuo* performance, and martial arts meet with an enthusiastic reception from spectators. The City God Temple Sacrificial Ceremony and Temple Fair at Wangqu Street in Chang'an District were listed among the first batch of the Intangible Cultural Heritage in Shaanxi Province.

1.18 侯官寨迎春社火牛老爷

The *Shehuo* Performance for Receiving the Lord Niu in Houguanzhai Village

陕西省西安市长安区侯官寨历史悠久，据《西安通览》记载，唐代已有此村。关于迎春社火牛老爷的由来，当地传说在清朝的时候，有一年立春那天，当地的县令偕同衙门里的同僚，去

Houguanzhai Village in Chang'an District, Xi'an City, Shaanxi Province, has a long history. As is recorded in *An Overview History of Xi'an* (*Xi'an tong lan*), the community has existed since the Tang Dynasty (618–907). As for the origin of the *Shehuo* Performance for the Lord Niu Heralding Spring, legend has it that during the Qing Dynasty (1636–1911), a local county magistrate went to countryside with his

乡下劝农及早准备春耕，县令还特意扶犁吆喝着牛在全县走了一圈。乡民们看到县令如此关心农事，倡导农业，大家的干劲都被鼓舞起来了，当年的春耕生产搞得热火朝天。乡民们为了纪念这位县令，便在侯官寨立祠祭祀，后来逐渐形成了迎春社火牛老爷。每年正月十五前后侯官寨耍社火时，社火队伍里就会出现一位骑在牛背上的十分突出的人物——牛老爷。这一习俗一直延续至今。侯官寨迎春社火牛老爷已列入陕西省第一批非物质文化遗产名录。

colleagues on the day of *Lichun*① to remind farmers to start preparations for the spring ploughing. He made a special point of driving farm cattle around the whole county. Greatly inspired by the county magistrate who was so concerned about agriculture, the farmers ploughed with relish that spring. The villagers set up a memorial temple in Houguanzhai Village in order to commemorate him. Later the *Shehuo* Performance for the Lord Niu Heralding Spring was gradually devised here. Every year around 15th January according to the Lunar Calendar, Houguanzhai Village holds acrobatic and pyrotechnic activities. One person is chosen by the villagers to dress like Lord Niu and ride the farm cattle among the performers. This tradition has been kept and carried on until the present day. The *Shehuo* Performance for the Lord Niu Heralding Spring in Houguanzhai Village was listed among the first batch of the Intangible Cultural Heritage in Shaanxi Province.

---

① The Chinese Lunar Calendar divides a year into 24 solar terms. *Lichun* is the first solar term. It begins when the Sun reaches the celestial longitude of 315° and ends when it reaches the longitude of 330°. In the Gregorian calendar, it usually begins around 4th February and ends around 18th February. It is also the beginning of a sexagenary cycle.

1.19 栎阳马踏青器山社火

The *Shehuo* Performance of Paper Horses Striding on a Porcelain Mountain in Yueyang Town

陕西省西安市临潼区栎阳镇的马踏青器山社火大约出现在明朝晚期。栎阳马踏青器山社火是民间社火中最复杂、最特殊的一种形式,仅流传于临潼栎阳镇西堡村。在表演马踏青器山社火时,还有秧歌、锣鼓、竹马、大头娃、高跷等表演以壮声势。每逢年节或庙会期间,栎阳就会有马踏青器山社火表演。

马踏青器山社火制作技艺高超,装扮程序复杂。首先要扎制成桩座,再将100多个彩色瓷碟固定在桩座上,形成青器山。最

The *Shehuo* Performance of Paper Horses Striding on a Porcelain Mountain first emerged around the time of the late Ming Dynasty (1368–1644) in Yueyang Town, Lintong District, Xi'an City, Shaanxi Province. As the most complicated and special form of acrobatics and pyrotechnics, Paper Horses Striding on a Porcelain Mountain is unique to Xibao Village in Yueyang Town, Lintong District. The *Shehuo* gains momentum through being staged in tandem with other performances, such as *yangge* dance, gong and drum routines, bamboo horses, people wearing big-headed masks, and stilt walking. During every Spring Festival or temple fair, Yueyang Town organises the spectacle of the *Shehuo* Performance of Paper Horses Striding on a Porcelain Mountain.

This performance is the product of excellent craftsmanship coupled with a complicated process of dressing the set and players. The principal steps are as follows: first, a pedestal is made; then, more than one hundred decorated porcelain plates are fixed onto the pedestal to

Pic. 13 *Shehuo* **Performance of Paper Horses Striding on a Porcelain Mountain**
Illustrated by Mathew Russell

后用铁架制成，并将彩色纸装扮起来的两匹马分别安装在青器山上的左右两端，让化装好的儿童骑在有坐垫的马背上，并与伸出马背的支架绑好。至此，整个马踏青器山的芯子便装扮完成。"险、奇、美"是其最突出的特点。其手工技艺为当地赵氏家族传承。栎阳马踏青器山社火已列入陕西省第一批非物质文化遗产名录。

simulate the so-called Porcelain Mountain; finally, two horses made from iron armatures and wrapped in coloured paper are installed on the left and right ends of the mountain. When two child players dressed up like characters from Shaanxi Opera are seated on cushions above the horse and tethered to a frame that extends out from the back of the horse, the *Xinzi* is ready for the performance. "Peril, peculiarity and beauty" are the hallmarks of this spectacle. The Zhao family are the custodians of the craftsmanship in the village. The *Shehuo* Performance of Paper Horses Striding on Porcelain Mountain in Yueyang Town was listed among the first batch of the Intangible Cultural Heritage in Shaanxi Province.

1.20 户县社火

The *Shehuo* Performance in Hu County

户县（今鄠邑）社火是从当地遗存的古代祭祀土地之神——社公的灵鼓祭祀仪式演变而来的。户县的社坛始建于西周初年，是户县社火起源之根。每年春节期间，陕西省西安市户县的许多村镇都会组织民间社火巡演活动。每隔两年，全县要组织一次春节大型民间艺术展演活动，而社火在展演活动中是最受群众欢迎的艺术形式之一。

户县社火是融民间舞蹈、民间音乐、民间美术、民间手工纸扎技艺等于一体的综合性艺术形式，主要有平台社火、芯子社火、马社火、高跷等。

The *Shehuo* Performance in Hu County (present-day Huyi District) is a traditional folk recreational activity that evolved from the sacrificial drum ceremony of the Duke of *She* (*She Gong*), the God of the Earth, in Hu County. The altar for the deity of *She* in Hu County, built in the early years of the Western Zhou Dynasty (1046 BC–771 BC), is the original root from which the *Shehuo* performance sprouted and grew. During the Spring Festival, folk acrobatic and pyrotechnic parades are held throughout the villages and towns of Hu County, Xi'an City, Shaanxi Province. Meanwhile, a large-scale biennial folk art exhibition replete with various kinds of performance are staged during the same period. Among them, the *Shehuo* performance is one of the most popular.

Integrating folk dances, folk music, folk arts, and handmade paper crafts, the Hu County *Shehuo* Performance is a synthesis of various art forms, including platform *Shehuo*, *Shehuo* Performance on *Xinzi* (child players from the villages standing on *Xinzi* frames made out of steel), Equestrian *Shehuo* Performance (village

其中尤以户县乔家庄的背社火最具特色。

players riding on horses), Stilt *Shehuo* (village players walking on stilts) and so forth. Among them, the *Shehuo* Performance of Balancing Acrobatics (performers from the village carry a steel frame or rig on which children from the community apparently balance) in Qiaojia Village is the most unique one.

户县社火历久弥新，具有旺盛的生命力和巨大的艺术魅力。户县社火已列入陕西省第一批非物质文化遗产名录。

Having been in existence for such a long time, the Hu County *Shehuo* Performance still maintains its vitality and great artistic charm. The Performance was listed among the first batch of the Intangible Cultural Heritage in Shaanxi Province.

1.21 蒋村正月民俗活动

The Folk Custom Activities in the First Lunar Month in Jiang Village

蒋村正月民俗活动是陕西省西安市户县蒋村的一种传统民间春节欢庆形式，每年从春节开始，历时一个月之久。蒋村正月民俗活动规模宏大，内容丰富，形式多样。主要的活动形式有社火、春官、歪

The Folk Custom Activities in the First Lunar Month in Jiang Village, Hu County, Xi'an City, Shaanxi Province, constitute a traditional method of celebrating Spring Festival. They commence at Lunar New Year and last for as long as a month. The Folk Custom Activities are carried out on a large scale, being rich in content and taking various forms. Its main activities include the *Shehuo* performance,

官、蛮鼓、板对等。

　　蒋村正月民俗活动形成于清代康熙初年,在数百年的历史发展过程中,其内容和形式不断丰富。蒋村正月民俗活动承载了许多重要的历史和文化信息,如社火是始于先秦、盛于唐宋的古老民俗活动形式的延续和发展;春官有始自周代的迎春习俗的烙印;歪官有唐代参军戏的结构和表现特点;蛮鼓是古代战鼓在民俗活动中的遗存;板对则是产生于明代的一种艺术形式在民俗活动中的传承。可以说,蒋村正月民俗活动是我国古代

Chunguan Opera,[①] *Waiguan* Opera,[②] the Barbarian Drum Competition, and the Couplet Challenge.

These practices in Jiang Village took shape in the early years of the Emperor Kangxi of Qing Dynasty(1662−1722). Through the course of hundreds of years of historical development, their content and form were perpetually enriched. The activities are rich in historical and cultural information. For example, the acrobatics and pyrotechnics have their source in ancient folk custom activities, which originated in the pre-Qin period and flourished in the Tang (618−907) and Song (960−1279) Dynasties. *Chunguan* Opera is characterised by the spring heralding customs since the Zhou Dynasty(1046 BC−256 BC), while *Waiguan* Opera shares structural and performance characteristics with the Administrator Opera (similar to crosstalk) of the Tang Dynasty. The Barbarian Drum Competition is the remnant of ancient war drum performances in a folk custom style. The Couplet Challenge is a popular

---

① *Chun* means "the Spring"; *Chunguan* is an epithet given to a minister of the Board of Rites. *Chunguan* Opera is the relics of the custom of Heralding Spring which dates back to the Zhou Dynasty (1046 BC−256 BC).
② *Waiguan* is commander-in-chief. *Waiguan* Opera concerns sending a document of appointment to the new commander-in-chief and this being read in front of his house.

民俗活动的"活化石",具有重要的历史价值、文化价值和研究价值。蒋村正月民俗活动已列入陕西省第一批非物质文化遗产名录。

activity with its roots in an artistic contest of the Ming Dynasty. It is therefore fair to say that the Folk Custom Activities in the First Lunar Month in Jiang Village are the "living fossils" of ancient Chinese folk activities, exhibiting important historical, cultural and research value. The Folk Custom Activities in the First Lunar Month in Jiang Village were listed among the first batch of the Intangible Cultural Heritage in Shaanxi Province.

1.22 陇州社火
The *Shehuo* Performance in Longzhou

陕西省宝鸡市陇县的陇州社火历史悠久,已有2000多年的历史。它是从上古祭祀土神的社日和祭祀火神的迎神赛会活动演变而来的,经世代传承,绵延至今。

陇州社火有马社火、背(陇县称"掣")社火、抬社火、山社火、车社火、芯子社火、高跷社火、秋千社火、跷板社火、步社火,还有舞狮、舞龙、

The *Shehuo* Performance in Longzhou, Long County, Baoji City, Shaanxi Province, has a long history stretching back more than 2,000 years. It evolved from ancient rites to worship the God of the Earth and the God of the Fire and has been passed down from generation to generation up to the present day.

Longzhou *Shehuo* Performance consists of more than 20 categories. These include the Equestrian *Shehuo* Performance, *Shehuo* Performance of Balancing Acrobatics, *Shehuo* Performance of Carrying Actors, *Shehuo* Performance on a Mountain (child players balance on steel frames fashioned to r

耍大头、古参军、杂耍、竹马、旱船、舞刀舞棍、秧歌舞、腰鼓舞等20多个种类。

陇州马社火威武雄壮，阵容庞大，气势磅礴。芯子社火、背社火、山社火、跷板社火、秋千社火造型玄妙，让人叹为观止。社火脸谱造型夸张，色彩浓烈，纹样奇特，简洁明快。在改革开放的今天，陇州社火这一民间艺术瑰宝焕发出新的艺术活力，成为重大节庆活动中最受群众欢迎的民间艺术形式之一。陇州社火已列入陕西

esemble mountains), Vehicle *Shehuo*, *Shehuo* Performance on *Xinzi*, *Shehuo* Performance on Stilts (walking on elongated artificial legs), *Shehuo* Performance on a Swing, *Shehuo* Performance on a Seesaw, Walking *Shehuo* Performance, and so forth. Besides the *Shehuo* performance itself, a festive flavour is added by activities including the lion dance, the dragon dance, big head play, Administrator Opera, juggling, bamboo horse-riding, dry boat, martial art show with sword, *yangge* dance, waist drum dance and so on.

The Equestrian *Shehuo* Performance is characterised by its power and large scale; the *Shehuo* Performance on *Xinzi*, the *Shehuo* Performance of Balancing Acrobatics, the *Shehuo* Performance on Mountain, the *Shehuo* Performance on a Seesaw and the *Shehuo* Performance on a Swing have mysterious styles which win awestruck praise from audiences. The facial makeup of the *Shehuo* performance is exaggerated and uses vibrant colours. Faces are painted in a peculiar fashion, being simple and bright. In the modern era of Reform and Opening Up, the Longzhou *Shehuo* Performance stands out as treasure of folk art, which has been infused with new artistic vitality and grown to become one of the most popular forms of folk

省第一批非物质文化遗产名录。

art in major festivals. The Longzhou *Shehuo* Performance was listed among the first batch of the Intangible Cultural Heritage in Shaanxi Province.

1.23 东峪孝歌
The Mourning Song of Dongyu

东峪孝歌主要流传于陕西省渭南市华县高塘镇东峪村。相传东峪孝歌迄今已有近400年的历史。孝歌也叫孝歌戏、挽歌、丧歌。在演唱孝歌过程中，伴奏和演唱交叉进行，伴奏乐器有大锣、大钹、小钹等。

东峪孝歌原本是殡葬仪中的一种悼念活动。在长期的演变过程中，孝歌的内容得到了很大的发展，逐渐形成了以守灵、悼念、孝敬、育人、娱乐和承志为内容，以歌奏、哀悼活动为载体，含有丰富民俗文化内容的民间礼

The Dongyu mourning song is mainly to be found around Dongyu Village, Gaotang Town, Hua County, Weinan City, Shaanxi Province. It is said that the Dongyu mourning song has a history of almost 400 years. A mourning song can also be referred to as mourning opera, a dirge or elegy. A mourning song is sung to the alternating accompaniment of instruments such as big gongs, big cymbals and small cymbals.

Originally the Dongyu mourning song was a kind of mourning activity which formed part of the funeral ritual. Through the course of its long evolution, the content of the mourning song has been greatly enriched and gradually embraced elements of folk etiquette including singing mourning songs with music and other mourning activities with the purposes of keeping vigil beside the coffin, mourning, displaying filial piety and educating offspring, etc. The principal

仪活动。东峪孝歌的主要剧目有《二十四孝》《杨家将》等。

东峪孝歌是劳动人民智慧的结晶,寄寓着中华民族的传统美德,具有重要的文化价值。东峪孝歌已列入陕西省第一批非物质文化遗产名录。

arias of Dongyu mourning song include *Twenty-four Filial Exemplars* (*Er shi si xiao*)① and *Generals of the Yang Family* (*Yang jia jiang*).②

The Dongyu Mourning Song represents the crystallisation of artisan wisdom. It embodies the traditional virtues of the Chinese nation and possesses important cultural value. The Dongyu Mourning Song was listed among the first batch of the Intangible Cultural Heritage in Shaanxi Province.

1.24 铁里芯子
Tieli *Xinzi*

芯子是民间工匠在精心设计的木质或铁质框架上,根据所表现的故事内容和预先设定的规格,彩饰成亭台楼阁、石桥彩虹、山川云端、花草树木等。其制

Xinzi are wooden or iron frames fashioned and decorated by artisan craftsmen to meet the specifications called for by particular plots. They may take the form of pavilions, stone bridges, rainbows, mountains, valleys, clouds, flowers and trees, to name but a few. They are exquisitely designed with beautiful shapes and

---

① *Twenty-four Filial Exemplars*, also translated as *Twenty-four Paragons of Filial Piety*, is a classic text of Confucian filial piety written by Guo Jujing during the Yuan Dynasty (1271–1368). The text was extremely influential in the medieval Far East and was used to teach Confucian moral values.

② The story of the *Generals of the Yang Family*, particularly its female generals, in the Song-Khitan wars of the late 10th and early 11th centuries, was a perennial favourite on the Chinese stage in the 19th and 20th centuries.

brilliant colours. The actors who balance on the *Xinzi* are mostly children between the ages of 5 or 6 and 11 or 12. They dress up as characters from Shaanxi Opera, historical stories, or fairytales, and are firmly tethered onto the main iron *Xinzi*, that is to say the iron pole that protrudes from the pedestal. Suspended in the air, they appear to tread on stylised clouds, leaves or branches, creating a magical and thrilling artistic spectacle. The Tieli *Xinzi* is mainly to be found around Tieli Village, Gaotang Town, Hua County, Weinan City, Shaanxi Province.

According to seasoned artisans, the Tieli *Xinzi* has a history that extends back nearly 400 years. Every year during Spring Festival or at major celebrations, local people in Tieli Village invariably perform *Xinzi*, an indispensable part of the *Shehuo* performance. Any *Shehuo* team capable of performing the Tieli *Xinzi* is especially welcomed and praised by the masses.

As its heirs slowly pass away, there is a great shortage of masters skilled in the techniques of producing the Tieli *Xinzi*. This

缺,铁里芯子已处于后继乏人的濒危状态,急需抢救。铁里芯子已列入陕西省第一批非物质文化遗产名录。

urgent situation calls for drastic measures to save a threatened art form. The Tieli *Xinzi* was listed among the first batch of the Intangible Cultural Heritage in Shaanxi Province.

1.25 陈炉窑神庙春秋祭祀礼仪
The Spring and Autumn Sacrificial Rites at the Chenlu Kiln Temple

位于陕西省铜川市印台区的陈炉窑神庙有着千年历史,从唐贞观二年(628)至民国累计重修了17次。陈炉窑神庙原有五通碑文,记述了陈炉的制瓷历史和窑神庙的功能与内涵。

陈炉窑神庙在每年的农历正月二十(民间传说这一天为窑神生日)和八月十五有两次社祭活动,每次三天,祭祀礼仪既庄重肃穆又热闹非凡。每逢祭祀时,陈炉东三社和西八

Located in Yintai District, Tongchuan City, Shaanxi Province, the Chenlu Kiln Temple has a history of more than one thousand years. It has been renovated a total of 17 times since the second year of the Zhenguan regnal era (627–649) in the Tang Dynasty to the Republic of China period. The Chenlu Kiln Temple bears five inscriptions describing the history of Chenlu porcelain and the function and connotation of the kiln temple.

The Chenlu Kiln Temple holds two patronage festivals per annum, namely on 20th January (the legendary birth date of the Kiln God) and on 15th August according to the Lunar Calendar. Both of these lasts for three days and the sacrificial rites are solemn and lively. When offering their sacrifices, residents from Three Associations in the east and Eight Associations

社的居民敲锣打鼓，抬着猪、羊等贡品分批祭祀，在鞭炮声中由主持人宣读祭文，按礼仪上香、焚表、三叩首，祈祷窑神保佑陈炉陶业兴旺，万民安康。

社祭之后，陶工三五成群地进行个人祭祀。每次社祭大戏连演三天三夜，各村社均有各具特色的社火表演以娱窑神。之后，社火队分赴陈炉各处巡回游演，异乡亲朋也来陈炉观赏祭祀盛典。陈炉窑神庙春秋祭祀礼仪已列入陕西省第一批非物质文化遗产名录。

in the west of Chenlu beat gongs and drums and carry their tributes, such as pigs and sheep to sacrifice in batches. To the sound of firecrackers, the host reads out the elegiac address, offers incense, burns written vows and kowtows three times according to the etiquette. The host prays to the Kiln God to bless the ceramics industry of Chenlu with prosperity and maintain the well-being of all the people.

After the communal sacrifice, the potters carry out the individual sacrifices in groups of three or five. Every time the communal festival drama is enacted it lasts for three days and three nights on end, and each village community has a unique *Shehuo* performance with which to entertain the Kiln God. After that, the *Shehuo* performing troupes will process around Chenlu and friends from other counties will also come to Chenlu to watch the ceremony. The Spring and Autumn Sacrificial Rites at the Chenlu Kiln Temple was listed among the first batch of the Intangible Cultural Heritage in Shaanxi Province.

1.26 耀州火亭子
The Fire Pavilion in the Yaozhou Area

陕西省铜川市耀州火亭子,也称火芯子,是一种民间社火表演艺术形式。它起源于清末,每年在正月十五元宵佳节的夜晚进行游演。火亭子以桌为台,每台一个故事,内容大多为戏剧故事和神话传说。除故事人物由儿童扮演外,其他景物均由纸扎彩绘的各式

The Yaozhou Fire Pavilion in Tongchuan City, Shaanxi Province, is also known as the Fire *Xinzi*. It is a carnivalesque example of *Shehuo* performance. Since late Qing Dynasty, people have staged a procession on the evening of Lantern Festival, the 15th day of the first month according to the Lunar Calendar. The fire pavilion takes a table as its stage, and each table displays one story, the main content of which is derived from drama stories and myths and legends. The characters in the story are played by children, while various coloured

Pic. 14 *Liu Hai Plays with a Golden Toad* Illustrated by Mathew Russell

彩灯装饰而成。其传统节目有《刘海戏金蟾》《麻姑献寿》《五福捧寿》等。

耀州火亭子制作工艺融绘画、纸扎等为一体，采用竹篾、铁丝或钢筋扎成各种艺术造型的灯具骨架，经裱糊涂染后即告完成。表演时，火亭子内燃蜡烛，灿烂绚丽，流光溢彩，彩灯和人物表演交相辉映。耀州火亭子在全国民间社火艺术中独树一帜，具有很高的艺术观赏价值。由于近年来耀州社火表演活动减少，火亭子制作工艺已处于濒危状态，亟待保护。耀州火亭子已列入陕西省第一批非物质文化遗产名录。

lantern lights decorated and covered in painted paper provide the other stage props. Its traditional programme include *Liu Hai Plays with the Golden Toad*, *Magu Offers Birthday Gifts*, and *Five Bats*① *Encircle the Character Shou*.

The Yaozhou Fire Pavilion is created by painting and binding different pieces of paper in succession. After the skeleton of the lantern has been fashioned from bamboo, wire or steel, people furnish and colour it with paper. Hence the fire pavilion is made. During the performance, candles are lit in the fire pavilion giving off a brilliant and vibrant appearance, with lanterns and character performances complementing one another in their radiance and beauty. The Yaozhou Fire Pavilion is unique among the arts of *Shehuo* performance and its aesthetic value is greatly appreciated. Owing to the decline of the Yaozhou *Shehuo* performance in recent years, the special process whereby fire pavilions are produced has become endangered and requires protection. The Yaozhou Fire Pavilion was listed among the first batch of the Intangible Cultural Heritage in Shaanxi Province.

---

① The Chinese word for "Bat" is *Bianfu*. Fu resembles "福" (literally "blessings") in pronunciation. Therefore it is always used by Chinese people in wishing others a blessed life.

1.27 勉县武侯墓清明祭祀活动

The Qingming Sacrificial Rite at the Wuhou Temple in Mian County

陕西省汉中市勉县武侯墓清明祭祀活动的前身为武侯墓清明文化庙会,它是陕南最大的古文化庙会活动,至今已延续近2000年之久。在诸葛亮葬于勉县定军山下后,各地百姓纷纷私祭于道陌之上。公元263年,后主刘禅近墓立祠,为诸葛亮修建了第一座祠庙(今武侯墓庙宇),同时规定"凡亲属、臣吏、百姓祭武侯者皆限至庙,断其私祭,以崇正礼",于是

The Qingming Sacrificial Rite at the Wuhou Temple (the Memorial Temple to the Marquis Wu) is enacted in Mian County, Hanzhong City, Shaanxi Province. It was formerly known as the Wuhou Tomb Qingming Cultural Temple Fair. This is the largest ancient cultural temple fair in southern Shaanxi Province and has a history extending back nearly two thousand years. After Zhuge Liang[①] was buried at the foot of Mount Dingjun[②] in Mian County, people from all over the country began the tradition of paying homage spontaneously on the roads near where they lived. In 263, King Liu Chan ordered the construction of a temple for Zhuge Liang (what is now the Wuhou Temple). Meanwhile, he stipulated that "in order to

---

① Zhuge Liang, courtesy name Kongming, was a Chinese statesman and military strategist. He was chancellor and later regent of the state of Shu Han (221−263) during the Three Kingdoms Period (220−280).
② Situated across Tiandang Mountain, it is separated by the River Hanjiang, and stands close to the old Yangping Pass. The mountain is eponym for the Battle of Mount Dingjun, fought between the warlords Liu Bei and Cao Cao in 219. The battle signified the only major territorial change between the Three Kingdoms in the whole period, with Liu Bei taking Hanzhong Commandery.

人们在每年清明时来到武侯墓扫墓，在武侯祠祭庙的礼仪由此开始。

据成书于清道光年间的《忠武侯祠墓志》记载，清明前一日为官祭筹备日。清明日参祭的各级官员身着朝服等候，由承祭官签祝文后，典仪（司仪人员）开始按仪宣读祭祀项目，逐步进行。现由于时代的变迁和人们思想观念的变化等多种因素，武侯墓清明祭祀活动已很简单、随意，不及记载的完整、庄重。勉县武侯墓清明祭祀活动已列入陕西省第一批非物质文化遗产名录。

establish a formal memorial rite, relatives, courtiers, and the masses alike can only worship his memory in the temple and all private or local sacrifices are forbidden". Therefore, people sweep clean the Wuhou Tomb every year during Qingming Festival. This marks the start of the ceremony at the Wuhou Temple.

The day before Qingming Festival is the preparation day for the official rites, according to the book entitled *The Epitaph of the Loyal Marquis' Temple* written during the reign of the Emperor Daoguang of Qing (1821–1850). Officials from all levels who participated in the Qingming sacrificial rite would wait to one side in their courtly attire. An officer in charge of the ceremony would sign an elegiac address. Then the event host read the order of ceremony to be followed as per the etiquette. With the passage of time, the evolution of people's mindsets and other factors, the Qingming sacrificial activities at the Wuhou Temple have become very much simpler and more extemporised, less comprehensive and solemn than those on record. The Qingming Sacrificial Rite at the Wuhou Temple in Mian County was listed among the first batch of the Intangible Cultural Heritage in Shaanxi Province.

2 陕西省第二批
非物质文化遗产名录中的民俗

The Folk Culture in the
Second Batch of the Intangible Cultural
Heritage in Shaanxi Province

2.1 西安都城隍庙民俗

Folk Custom at the Xi'an Metropolitan City God Temple [①]

西安都城隍庙坐落于陕西省西安市西大街中段。西安都城隍庙始建于明洪武二十年（1387），明宣德八年（1433）由东门里移建于现址，迄今已有600多年历史。西安是城隍信仰的发源地和传播地。

西安都城隍庙民俗主要有祭祀仪式和城隍庙会两项。西安都城隍庙的道场祭祀分为阳事道场和阴事

The Xi'an Metropolitan City God Temple (Chenghuang [②] Temple) is currently located in the middle section of West Avenue, Xi'an City, Shaanxi Province. First built in the 20th year (1387) of the reign of the Emperor Hongwu of Ming, it was moved to its present site from the East Gate of the city in the 8th year (1433) of the reign of the Emperor Xuande of Ming. In other words, it has a history of more than 600 years. Xi'an was the birthplace and cradle of City God worship.

The principal folk customs of the Xi'an Metropolitan City God Temple include a sacrificial rite and a temple fair. The Taoist sacrificial rite at the temple is held on two kinds of occasions, namely, events pertaining

---

① Higher in level than ordinary City God Temples at provincial or county level, the Xi'an Metropolitan God Temple is one of the four of its kind within China, with the other three being respectively in Beijing, Nanjing and Wugong (in Shaanxi Province). The Xi'an Metropolitan God Temple embraces all the City God Temples in northwestern China.

② *Cheng* refers to the ancient Chinese defensive rampart of the city, while *Huang* is the literal meaning of a moat, an ancient Chinese method of protecting the city. The *Chenghuang* was believed to provide divine protection for the physical defense of the city, especially the walls and moats surrounding it.

道场。阳事道场是为活着的人举行的消灾解难、祈福延寿等的仪式，一般持续三天。阴事道场是为超度久处阴司的亡魂，使其超升仙界的仪式，一般也是持续三天。道场安排不是一成不变的，可根据法事内容的不同进行适当调整。

西安都城隍庙在每年农历正月初一、十五，四月初八、八月中秋是传统庙会，会期为三天。六月十九为圣诞、神诞节祭祖盛会，此外还定期举行酬神戏会。而新春祈福庙会盛况空前，动辄有数十万人参加。新春庙会中有许多民间传统活动，如送春联、祭城隍、迎财神、烧新年头炉香等。也有秦腔、高跷、社火、民间绝活、鼓乐演奏等丰富多彩的民间艺

to the *Yang* and those pertaining to the *Yin*. The *Yang* Taoist rites are held for the benefit of the living, praying for blessings and longevity. Such ceremonies generally last for three days; while the *Yin* Taoist rites benefit the dead, aiming to release the souls of the deceased from hell so they can pass into heaven. These last for three days apiece. The arrangements or procedures for both kinds of ceremony are not set in stone. They can be adjusted in accordance with the purpose of the worship.

Xi'an Metropolitan City God Temple Fairs always last for three days and are staged four times a year, falling on the first day and the 15th day of the lunar January, the 8th day of the lunar April and at Mid-Autumn Festival. On the 19th day of the lunar June, the birthday of holy spirits and gods, ceremonies are held to pay reverence to ancestors. In addition, operas will be performed to give thanks to the immortals. The Chinese New Year's Blessings-Praying Temple Fair sees unprecedented pomp, with hundreds of thousands of people coming to attend. There are many traditional folk components to the temple fair, such as sending spring couplets, offering sacrifices to the Metropolitan City God, welcoming the God of Fortune, burning the first incense, etc. During

表演。西安都城隍庙民俗已列入陕西省第二批非物质文化遗产名录。

the temple fair, there are also Shaanxi Opera performances, stilt-walking, acrobatics and pyrotechnics, displays of unique folk skills, drum performances and other colourful folk art spectacles. The folk customs of the Xi'an Metropolitan City God Temple Fair were listed among the second batch of the Intangible Cultural Heritage in Shaanxi Province.

2.2 西安大白杨社火芯子

The *Shehuo* Performance on *Xinzi* in Grand Baiyang Village, Xi'an City

陕西省西安市未央区大白杨村社火芯子历史悠久，是东周以来傩文化的延续。大白杨社火芯子形式多样，内容丰富，其中芯子表演是大白杨社火的主体，也是大白杨村社火中最有影响、最具魅力的艺术形式。

The *Shehuo* Performance on *Xinzi* in Grand Baiyang Village, Weiyang District, Xi'an City, Shaanxi Province, has a long history, evolving from the culture of exorcism named *nuo*[①] sacrifice, also known as the *nuo* ceremony, found in the Eastern Zhou Dynasty (770 BC–256 BC). The *Shehuo* Performance on *Xinzi* in Grand Baiyang Village are various in form and rich in content. The *Xinzi* itself is the centrepiece and regarded as the most influential and charming

---

① *nuo* was originally a type of sacrificial and magical ritual held to expel evil spirits and pestilence. Its name is derived from one of such rituals, where people shouted "*nuo*, *nuo*" to drive away the devil.

大白杨社火芯子一般由2~4个四五岁的小孩扮演，依靠从底座中伸出的那根叫芯子的铁条将孩子支撑起来，高悬空中，从表面上看不出有立脚之处，险中求趣的特点令人叹为观止。表演的内容大多为戏曲故事、神话传说、民间故事、历史人物故事等。

大白杨社火芯子是集民间戏剧、音乐、舞蹈、美术、手工纸扎和锻造技艺于一体的大型综合性艺术形式和动静结合的立体造型艺术形式。它雅俗共赏，能够满足不同文化层次群众的欣赏要求。大白杨社火芯子是当地春节期间不可缺少的大型表演项目，承载着中华民族优秀的传统文化血脉，是当地农村人文环境、民情风俗、群

component. The performance is acted out by 2 to 4 village children between the ages of 4 or 5. They are firmly tethered to the iron *Xinzi*. That is to say the iron pole that protrudes from the pedestal. Suspended up high, they appear to tread on thin air, creating a magical and thrilling artistic spectacle which wins praise and admiration from the audience. The contents of the performance are mostly drawn from Shaanxi Opera, fairytales, folk stories, or historical stories.

The *Shehuo* Performance on *Xinzi* in Grand Baiyang Village is a large-scale comprehensive art and the stereoscopic styling art form with a combination of dynamic and static elements that embrace folk opera, music, dance, fine arts, handmade paper crafts and forging techniques. It caters to a broad audience, tantalising both refined and popular tastes. As a large-scale performance indispensable to Spring Festival, this performance on *Xinzi* in Grand Baiyang Village carries forward the outstanding traditional culture of the Chinese nation. It is a living treasure house of the local rural cultural environment, folk customs and group ideology. The *Shehuo* Performance on *Xinzi* in Grand Baiyang Village was listed among the second

体意识的活态风俗宝库。西安大白杨社火芯子已列入陕西省第二批非物质文化遗产名录。

batch of the Intangible Cultural Heritage in Shaanxi Province.

2.3 户县北乡迎祭城隍民俗活动

The City God Collection and Veneration Ceremony in Northern Hu County

户县北乡迎祭城隍民俗活动是流传于陕西省西安市户县北部乡村的古老民俗活动，早在明代中叶就

The City God Collection and Veneration Ceremony is always held in rural areas of northern Hu County. It is an ancient folk activity which was practiced uninterrupted for hundreds of years, from its origins in the

Pic. 15　The City God Shrine Illustrated by Mathew Russell

已非常盛行。自明代中叶至民国末年，迎祭城隍活动一脉相承，数百年来未曾中断。民国三十七年（1948），户县县政府曾以"勤俭建国"的名义明令禁止这一活动，新中国成立后恢复，1957年以迷信活动再次被禁止。1987年后民间自发恢复了这一民俗活动，年年迎送，直至今日。

户县北乡迎祭城隍民俗活动的形式古老、隆重而盛大。迎神队伍举村参与，长达数里。它由神职队和民间艺术表演组成。神职队围绕城隍夫妇神轿，武官陪护，文官相随，道教乐队前导，拈香诵经队伍尾随。神物祭器、神前仪仗一应俱全。民间艺术表演有百面锣鼓、梆子舞、夹板舞、芯

middle of the Ming Dynasty to the final year of the Republic of China period. In the 37th year of the Republic of China, it was banned by the county government for the sake of saving funds to rejuvenate the nation and resumed after the People's Republic of China was founded in 1949. It was banned again in 1957 as a superstitious activity. After 1987, local people in Hu County spontaneously revived this folk custom and have celebrated it ever since.

The City God Collection and Veneration Ceremony in northern Hu County is ancient and solemn in character with a streak of pomp. The groups or configurations of *Yingshen* (Gods collecting from temples in a village) stretch for miles and include almost every last villager. Clerics and folk art performers have their own groups. The clergy formation surrounds the sedan chair in which the City God Couple sits. The two sides of the sedan are flanked by military officers, followed by civilian officials. In front of the sedan a Taoist band leads the way, with a cluster offering incense and chanting scriptures behind them. In the midst

2 陕西省第二批非物质文化遗产名录中的民俗
The Folk Culture in the Second Batch of the Intangible Cultural Heritage in Shaanxi Province

Pic. 16 *Bangzi* Dancing Illustrated by Mathew Russell

子社火、马社火、武术杂耍和旱船竹马等。整个队伍以旌旗仪仗为前导，报马奔驰穿梭，锣鼓震天动地，社火异彩纷呈，绵延数里，成为声势浩大的民间艺术盛典。交接神像时，迎送双方要以古法举行祭祀仪式，并举行盛大的民间艺术祭祀表演。

of the parade, people can observe offertory items, sacrificial utensils, and guards of honour. Folk art performances include the hundred-face gongs and drums, the *Bangzi* dancing (a dance performed with two wooden sticks in each hand), the plywood dancing (a dance in which a plywood board is beaten), the *Shehuo* Performance on *Xinzi*, the Equestrian *Shehuo* Performance, martial arts juggling, land boat-paddling and bamboo hobbyhorse dancing, etc. The parade is led by guards of honour with flags held aloft. Messengers on horseback shuttle back and forth among the crowd. Gongs and drums make such a deafening sound that it might shake the heavens and the earth. The magnificent *Shehuo* performance of acrobatics groups stretches for miles, making an impressive display of ceremonial folk art. During the handing-over and collection of the god statues, ancient sacrificial rites and grand folk art displays are held at the village the statues depart from and the village in which they arrive.

The faith of collecting the City God and the relevant sacrificial rites are inherited collectively by *She* (associations or societies), with every association as a unit. The sacrificial issues in the three City God societies are co-ordinated by the City God Association General. When a village takes its turn to host the ceremony, a council will be selected to oversee the specific details of that year's event. The City God Collection and Veneration Ceremony in Northern Hu County integrate rich contents, such as folk faith, religious sacrificial rites, folk customs, folk art etc. It is therefore regarded as a living fossil, significant for research into religious culture, folk culture and folk art. The City God Collection and Veneration Ceremony in Northern Hu County was listed among the second batch of the Intangible Cultural Heritage in Shaanxi Province.

户县北乡迎城隍信仰和祭祀礼仪是以社为单位集体传承下来的。三个城隍社都由城隍总会协调迎祭城隍有关事宜，迎神的村子也会在当年设立理事会，负责迎神具体事项。户县北乡迎祭城隍民俗活动包含了民间信仰、宗教祭祀礼仪、民俗和民间艺术等多种内容，是研究宗教文化、民俗文化、民间艺术的活化石。户县北乡迎祭城隍民俗活动已列入陕西省第二批非物质文化遗产名录。

2.4 楼观台祭祀老子礼仪

The Sacrificial Etiquette for the Veneration of Laozi at Louguantai Temple in Zhouzhi County

位于陕西省西安市周至县的楼观台被誉为"道教祖庭圣地"和"道文化发祥地"。我国春秋时的大思想家、道家的创始人李聃（老子）在这里留下了享誉海内外的哲学巨著《道德经》。3000 年来，基于《道德经》的重大影响，历代有 60 余位帝王在楼观台建造了数十处殿、亭、楼、塔祭祀老子，形成了有皇家参与的具有特殊文化色彩的楼观台祭祀老子礼仪，并延续至今。

楼观台祭祀老子礼仪有皇家或国家祭

Louguantai Temple, located in Zhouzhi County, Xi'an City, Shaanxi Province, is known as the "Holy Land of Taoism" and the "Birthplace of Taoist Culture". During the Spring and Autumn Period (770 BC–476 BC), Li Dan, also known as Laozi, the great ideologist and originator of Taoism, wrote his internationally-renowned philosophical masterpiece entitled the *Tao Te Ching*① on this very site. Over the past 3,000 years, more than sixty emperors have been moved by the influence of the *Tao Te Ching* and built dozens of temples, pavilions, buildings, and towers with the purpose of worshipping Laozi. These collectively form a unique cultural sacrificial ceremony (sanctioned by ancient royalty) which has been passed down to the present day.

There are three types of etiquette involved in offering sacrifices to Laozi at the Louguantai

---

① The *Tao Te Ching* is a Chinese classic text traditionally credited to the 6th-century BC sage Laozi. It provides the basis for the philosophical school of Taoism, which is an important pillar of Chinese thought.

Pic. 17　Animal Sacrifice Illustrated by Mathew Russell

祀、民间祭祀和宗教祭祀三种类型。皇家或国家机构祭祀，依次的步骤是鸣奏黄钟大吕、表演国宾舞、主持人通读祭文、全体祭祀人员行祭拜礼、在音乐伴奏中列队绕场依次退散；民间祭祀的步骤依次是锣鼓及鼓乐演奏、献大蜡及纸活、诵经、进香祭拜、龙舞表演、散祭；宗教祭祀的步骤是先

Temple, namely royal or national sacrifice, folk sacrifice and religious sacrifice. Royal or national sacrifices are performed according to the following steps: playing solemn music, performing state-guest-heralding or welcoming dance, the host reading a funeral oration, and all the company present bowing and retreating to musical accompaniment. The steps for folk sacrifices are, in order: a gong and drum performance, offering candles of large size as well as sacrificial objects made out of paper, chanting, offering incense, a dragon dance and individual sacrifice. Religious sacrifices include the following steps: selecting an auspicious

选择黄道吉日，沐浴斋戒，设置祭坛，请主进位，道士立于其左右并上香，吉时升坛，俯拜上表，道众同拜，以表诚意，宣读礼赞老子诗文，后参礼并依次上香行礼、诵咒。以上过程均伴有道乐演奏。近年来，国家对老子祭祀活动非常重视，先后多次举办了"楼观台老子文化周"活动和"九九重阳节公祭老子"活动等。民间祭祀活动更是规模宏大。楼观台祭祀老子礼仪已列入陕西省第二批非物质文化遗产名录。

day, followed by ablutions and an altar set up for the deity. Taoists stand on the two sides of the altar and then offer incense. The worship starts at the selected auspicious moment. All the assembled pilgrims and Taoists, bow to show their sincerity, followed by reading poems of praise to Laozi, burning incense and chanting scriptures. All the said steps are performed to Taoist musical accompaniment. In recent years, China has attached greater importance to offering sacrifices to Laozi, and a number of activities have been organised, such as the "the Louguantai Temple Laozi Cultural Week", and the "Double Ninth Festival Public Sacrifice to Laozi", etc. Folk sacrificial activities have also been staged on a larger scale. The Sacrificial Etiquette for the Veneration of Laozi at Louguantai Temple was listed among the second batch of the Intangible Cultural Heritage in Shaanxi Province.

2.5 华夏财神故里祭祀活动

The Sacrificial Activities to Worship the God of Wealth in His Hometown

华夏财神祭祀起源于陕西省西安市周

The sacrifice to the Chinese God of Wealth can be traced back to Zhaoda Village,

至县集贤镇赵大村。据周至旧县志记载:"华夏财神姓赵名朗,字公明,号玄坛元帅。邑东南方有赵大村,传为玄坛元帅故里。"赵公明因匡扶正义而受福禄寿三仙点化,他食桃为仙,主管人间钱财,民间敬之为财神。因此,当地祭拜赵公明的祭祀活动遂成为习俗,流传至今。

华夏财神祭祀礼仪一般在农历正月初一至正月十五及农历三月十五、六月初六、八月十五进行。祭祀

Jixian Town, Zhouzhi County, Xi'an City, Shaanxi Province. According to the *Annals of Zhouzhi County* (the first edition), "the Chinese God of Wealth is named Zhao Lang, with his courtesy name[①] Gongming and his style name Marshal Xuantan. There is a village called Zhaoda in the southeast of the city, which is said to be the hometown of Marshal Xuantan. Because of his righteousness, Zhao Gongming (Zhao Lang) was enlightened and transformed by three immortals—the God of Fortune, the God of Prosperity, and the God of Longevity—so that he became an immortal himself after eating peaches. He was designated to be in charge of wealth. He has been therefore respected by common people and regarded as the God of Wealth. Local sacrificial activities to worship Zhao Gongming have become a custom ever since.

The sacrificial ceremonies to the Chinese God of Wealth always take place three times a year, falling between the 1st day and the 15th day of the lunar January, the 15th day of the lunar March, the 6th day of the lunar June, and

---

① The courtesy name (*zi* 字) is bestowed upon one at adulthood in addition to one's given name. Formerly in China, the *zi* would replace a male's given name when he turned twenty, as a symbol of adulthood and respect.

2 陕西省第二批非物质文化遗产名录中的民俗
The Folk Culture in the Second Batch of the Intangible Cultural Heritage in Shaanxi Province

Pic. 18 The God of Wealth Illustrated by Mathew Russell

礼仪分敬神、迎神、求签、还神、送财气、财神舞等仪程。敬神即香客的上香活动，包括斋戒、净手、燃烛、上供、化钱、祈祷五个步骤；迎神即祈福、求财、消灾等活动；迎神后即求签；还神即谢神，就是在求签应验后向神还愿；送财气是指由一些祭拜者装扮成财神或抬上财神像，还有童男童女

the 15th day of the lunar August. The procedures to be worked through are: worshipping the God, welcoming the God, drawing divination sticks, reciprocating the God, the God delivering fortune to the people, followed by the God of Wealth dance. Worshipping the God means the pilgrims offering incense according to five specific steps: fasting, cleansing hands, lighting candles, offering sacrifices, burning ancestor money and praying. Welcoming the God means praying for blessings, asking for good fortune and disaster relief, followed by praying and drawing divination sticks. Reciprocating the God means offering up thanks to God's

各一人装扮成赐财童子,后有乐器锣鼓队组成送财气队伍,队伍每到一处门前,两赐财童子便手拿财神帖子口喊"财神到",并将神帖送至主人手中,主人来庙还愿;财神舞则是在祭拜时演出的一种大型舞蹈形式。

blessing after what the divination sticks drawn predict comes true. The process of the God delivering fortune proceeds thus: some people dress up like the God of Wealth or carry an effigy of him to visit households accompanied by two delivering-fortune children, a little girl and a little boy, together with a delivering-fortune team of gongs and drums. On arriving at the gate of a house, the two children shout "Here comes the God of Wealth" and raise up high a message written on paper. This they hand to the head of the household, who if the text comes true must visit the God of Wealth Temple and offer up thanks. The God of Wealth dance is performed in the course of the worship.

Pic. 19　Offering Incense Illustrated by Mathew Russell

华夏财神祭祀礼仪有着重要的历史价值和民俗研究价值。华夏财神故里祭祀活动已列入陕西省第二批非物质文化遗产名录。

The Sacrificial Rites to Worship the God of Wealth in His Hometown have great historical and folkloric research value. The Sacrificial Activities to Worship the God of Wealth in His Hometown were listed among the second batch of the Intangible Cultural Heritage in Shaanxi Province.

2.6 渭河南忙罢古会

The Ancient Slack-Season Gathering of Kith and Kin on the South Bank of the River Wei

渭河南忙罢古会是陕西省咸阳市秦都区渭河南岸87个自然村之间约定俗成的一种民间风俗活动。忙罢古会起于何时，现已无从查考。渭河南岸的农村，在农历六月和七月是一个相对松缓的时段，清闲下来的劳动者触发了彼此的思念之情，这就是渭河南忙罢古会产生的原因。渭河南忙罢古会于农历六月初一从秦都区的吴家庄开始，农历七月底在北槐村等村

The Ancient Slack-Season Gathering of Kith and Kin on the South Bank of the River Wei is a folk custom, unanimously practiced by the 87 villages, on the south bank of the River Wei in Qindu District, Xianyang City, Shaanxi Province. No historical materials can verify when this custom actually started. During the slack season (the 6th and 7th lunar months, namely June and August on the Western Calendar) when the farmers have relatively little to do, they miss their family members and friends. Thus begins the ancient gathering of kith and kin. The gathering commences on the 1st lunar day of June from Wujiazhuang Village in Qindu District, and concludes at the end of the lunar July in Beihuai and several

结束，前后历时两个月。其间，域内所有村庄皆按约定好的时间顺序依次过会，具体日期是固定的，多为单日，偶有双日。双日多定在农历初十、二十、三十这几天。渭河南忙罢古会走亲戚常带礼馍，因此也叫"蒸馍会"。渭河南忙罢古会还有一个讲究就是来客要全。这一天不但所有的亲戚都要来，而且要好的朋友也会登门。另一方面，渭河南忙罢古会也为男女青年说媒拉线提供了机会，因此也叫"女婿会"。

渭河南忙罢古会的另一个重要议程是待客、坐席、吃饭。传统的讲究是"早汤午席"两顿饭。早汤是浇汤揪面，午席是吃席面。同样是浇汤揪面，同样是摆桌设席，各家却不尽一样，主

other villages, lasting for two months in total. During the gathering, all villages hold their celebrations in a sequence agreed upon prior to the event. The dates of each year's gathering are fixed, mostly on odd-numbered days and occasionally on even-numbered days. The even-numbered days are usually the lunar 10th, the lunar 20th, and the lunar 30th days in those two months. The gathering is also called the "gathering of steamed buns" since relatives come to visit with "courtesy steamed buns", and other utensils. An important feature of this gathering lies in that on the day of gathering not only relatives are welcome to come, but also good friends are allowed to pay a visit. The gathering also provides opportunities for young people to meet and get to know each other, and even fall in love. Hence, the nickname "gathering of sons-in-law".

The most important content of the gathering is treating guests with two meals, traditionally called "morning soup and afternoon banquet". The "morning soup" is noodles with soup, while the "afternoon banquet" is called the "eating banquet" (bottles of liquor and dishes are served and presented on the banquet table). Although every family will treat guests to noodles with soup and a banquet of liquor and dishes, the

要依据主人的家境、财力、当年庄田的丰歉而定。但无论招待饭菜丰盛与否，客人都会从主人的殷勤与忙碌中感受到主人的真诚。旧时过会还讲究在村里请戏班唱戏。唱戏的筹办由各家族每年轮流担任，筹办人称为"会头"，负责张罗请戏、唱戏等事务。渭河南忙罢古会特色鲜明，历史悠久。渭河南忙罢古会已列入陕西省第二批非物质文化遗产名录。

quality of the fare varies. Some families are richer than others and that year's harvest may have been plentiful or poor. Regardless of the grade of the food served, guests will feel the sincerity of the host from their diligence and industry. In the old days, opera troupes were also invited to perform. Each clan or family in the village would take turns to oversee the preparation of the performance. The person in charge was called "head of the gathering", responsible for relevant specific issues. The Ancient Slack-Seaon Gathering of Kith and Kin on the South Bank of the River Wei has distinctive features and a long history. The gathering was listed among the second batch of the Intangible Cultural Heritage in Shaanxi Province.

2.7 长武庙宇泥塑礼仪
The Monastic Clay Sculptures of Changwu County

陕西省咸阳市长武县的庙宇泥塑产生于当地宗教信仰和民俗文化的基础之上，有着丰富的历史和精神文化内涵。长武庙宇泥塑在形体上站、坐、

The monastic clay sculptures of Changwu County in Xianyang City, Shaanxi Province are based on local religious beliefs and folk culture. They exhibit rich historical and spiritual cultural connotations. The monastic clay sculptures of Changwu County come in different models, including standing up, sitting down, lying and

卧、悬兼而有之，尺寸小到尺余，大至两丈。人物形象逼真，表情丰富，个性鲜明，具有独特的艺术风格和文化魅力。

长武庙宇泥塑以手工制作为主，忌用铁具。常用的工具有尺板、木刻刀、印图木模、修制木模等40多种，根据塑像部位装饰的需要也可临时制作一些工具。

长武庙宇泥塑工艺复杂，有筑神台、定位、制作木模架、绑草、和泥、涂泥、雕形、修饰、晾干、彩绘等工序，且要择吉

hanging, and are of different sizes, being as short as one *chi*[①], or as tall as two *zhang*[②]. The characters are lifelike. They feature rich facial expressions and have distinctive personalities, which endow them with a unique artistic style and cultural charm.

The monastic clay sculptures of Changwu County are mainly made by hand, with iron tools being strictly forbidden. More than 40 kinds of implements are allowed, such as wide rulers, wooden carving knives, wooden molds for printing, and wooden molds for remodelling, etc. Some makeshift tools can also be employed according to the decoration requirements of the statue.

The monastic clay sculptures of Changwu County are complex in workmanship. The process proceeds thus: a platform for styling deity figures is set up, postures are finalised, a wooden molding frame is made, straw is bound, mud-making, mud-painting, mud-sculpting,

---

① *Chi* is a traditional Chinese unit of length. One *chi* is equal to 0.33 metres. Its length was originally derived from the distance measured by a human hand, from the tip of the thumb to the tip of the forefinger, and is similar to the ancient span. It first appeared during China's Shang Dynasty approximately 3,000 years ago and has since been adopted by other East Asian countries.

② *Zhang*, an old Chinese measure of length equal to 10 *chi*, or 3.58 metres (11 feet 9 inches).

日开工。泥塑制作完成后要"点眼开光""通体开窍",举行隆重的吉庆典礼。

长武庙宇泥塑流传区域较广,是含有历史、宗教、民俗等多元文化内容的传统艺术形式,其产生和流传有着深刻的社会历史根源。长武庙宇泥塑礼仪已列入陕西省第二批非物质文化遗产名录。

decorating, drying in the air and painting, etc. It is necessary to start working on an auspicious day. After the clay sculpture is completed, a grand ceremony is held to draw the eyes of the deity to make it more lively.

The monastic clay sculpture is widespread across Changwu County. As a traditional art form, it contains manifold layers of connotations, religious, historical and folk culture. Its survival keeps alive deep social and historical roots. The Monastic Clay Sculptures of the Changwu County were listed among the second batch of the Intangible Cultural Heritage in Shaanxi Province.

2.8 蒲城罕井秋千民俗

The Swing Custom of Hanjing Town in Pucheng County

陕西省渭南市蒲城县的罕井秋千是当地独特的一种民间风俗活动,相传迄今已有600多年历史。其制作工艺、尺寸以及表演前的祭祀活动等都是有严格规定的。蒲城罕井秋千

The swing of Hanjing Town in Pucheng County, Weinan City, Shaanxi Province, is a unique folk custom activity that has been observed and practiced for more than 600 years. Strict stipulations govern the craftsmanship and size of the swing, together with the sacrificial activities which must be undertaken before the show. The Hanjing swing frame is usually made

Pic. 20 Swing-making Illustrated by Mathew Russell

在节日表演时一般是在白天扎制，子时扶立，清明时在社火的鞭炮锣鼓声中荡起。蒲城罕井秋千老少皆宜。老年人荡秋千百病不侵，延年益寿。青年人荡秋千则寓意着鲤跃龙门，前程无量。蒲城罕井秋千以高、飘、悠、巧、柔、美、欢而久负盛名，为人们所称道。一首在当地广为流传的古体诗描绘了荡秋千时的生动场景：

and decorated horizontally during the daytime, then erected vertically between 11 p.m. and 1 a.m. During Qingming Festival, the swing frame is adorned with firecrackers, gongs and drums. The Hanjing swing in Pucheng County appeals to all ages. Elderly people who ride the swings will have health and longevity. Young people who do likewise will have a bright future. The Hanjing swing of Pucheng County has long enjoyed a good reputation, being praised as high, floating, delicate, ingenious, soft and beautiful, as well as for the joyful ambience it creates. A well-known archaic poem depicts the vivid scene of swinging：

二八佳人美少年,	Boys and girls in their teens,
鸳鸯楼台戏秋千;	Swing in a yard like mandarin ducks.
红粉面对红粉面,	Powdered face to powdered face,
素玉肩对素玉肩;	Jade shoulder to jade shoulder.
两双玉手挽又挽,	Two jade hands take two jade counterparts,
四只金莲颠倒颠;	Four golden lotus feet swing backward and forward.
游春才子遥相指,	Pointed afar by gifted youth touring spring,
疑似飞仙下九天。	To be immortals descending from paradise.

Pic. 21　Hanjing Swing Illustrated by Mathew Russell

2008年7月，蒲城罕井秋千应邀在"中国渭南首届文化旅游节"上展示，以其独特的民俗特征深深地打动了成千上万观赏者的心灵。蒲城罕井秋千一直是以传统技艺形式进行表演，其制作方法等相关程序都原汁原味地保留了传统的风俗习惯和风貌。蒲城罕井秋千民俗已列入陕西省第二批非物质文化遗产名录。

In July 2008, the Hanjing swing of Pucheng County was exhibited by invitation at the "the first Cultural Tourism Festival in Weinan, China". Tens of thousands of viewers were touched by its distinct folk charisma. The Hanjing swing performance has always followed traditional techniques, and its production methods and relevant performing procedures have been well-protected, therefore retaining age-old customs and features. The Swing Custom of Hanjing Town, Pucheng County was listed among the second batch of the Intangible Cultural Heritage in Shaanxi Province.

2.9 渭北细狗撵兔竞技

The Contest of Chasing Rabbits with Greyhounds from North of the River Wei

陕西省渭南市蒲城县的细狗撵兔竞技历史悠久。汉代蒲城属皇室上林苑的一部分，司马相如在《上林赋》中有"兔园夹

The contest of chasing rabbits with greyhounds in Pucheng County, Weinan City, Shaanxi Province has a long history. Pucheng used to be one part of the Shanglin Imperial Park in the Han Dynasty (202 BC–220 CE). Sima Xiangru[①] (179 BC–118 BC), a Chinese

---

① Sima Xiangru is a significant figure in the history of classical Chinese poetry, and is generally regarded as the greatest of all composers of Chinese *fu* (赋) rhapsodies.

池水"的记述。唐皇室狩猎娱乐活动后来传入蒲城民间,逐渐演变为细狗撵兔的民间竞技活动。蒲城之细狗,乃渭北名犬。人们描绘它的形状:"黄瓜嘴,羊鼻梁,四蹄如蒜;腰似弓,腿似箭,耳垂尾卷。"蒲城细狗撵兔猎鼠,机智灵活,看家护院,极通人性,是人类的好朋友。

poet and politician who lived during the Western Han Dynasty, described in his *Rhapsody on the Shanglin Imperial Park* that "rabbits in the gardens thrive with pool water", implying the rabbit-hunting tradition was alive in the Tang Dynasty. The hunting and entertainments of the Tang royal family were later introduced into Pucheng County, gradually evolving into the chasing rabbits with greyhounds contest. The greyhounds of Pucheng County are famous among the dogs found to the north of the River Wei. People have reported how they possess, "A cucumber-shaped mouth, a distinctive nose bridge as high

Pic. 22　Greyhounds Chase Rabbits Illustrated by Mathew Russell

as sheep's, four hooves like garlic; a waist like a bow, legs like arrows, down-turned ears and a rolling tail." The Pucheng greyhounds are capable at chasing rabbits and hunting mice. They are witty, nimble and humane, so they can guard a household and be good friends with people.

The rabbit-chasing contest is regularly organised by greyhound enthusiasts during the slack season of every year. This activity mainly falls on Lantern Festival, Dragon Boat Festival and Laba Festival[①], etc. On that day, greyhound lovers from Pucheng County, its neighbouring counties or cities, and even from Xi'an City, and Shanxi, Gansu, and Henan provinces will dress and decorate their dogs with colourful habiliments. When the competition begins, the reins will be released and the dogs set free to gallop and chase. It is a spectacular scene especially with tens of thousands of people watching and exclaiming in surprise. The contest of chasing rabbits plays a positive role in bringing people together, reducing vermin,

---

① The twelfth month of the Chinese calendar is called the the *La* Month, hence the name "Laba Festival", a traditional Chinese holiday celebrated on the eighth day of the *La* Month, which was also the enlightenment day of the Buddha. Therefore, many customs of the Laba Festival are related to Buddhism. It is customary on this day to eat Laba Congee.

人们的团结意识，减少兽害，维护和谐生态环境有着积极意义。蒲城细狗撵兔竞技已列入陕西省第二批非物质文化遗产名录。

and maintaining a harmonious ecological environment. The Contest of Chasing Rabbits with Greyhounds in Pucheng County was listed among the second batch of the Intangible Cultural Heritage in Shaanxi Province.

2.10 跑骡车
Driving Mule Carts

跑骡车是陕西省渭南市民间社火的一种表演形式，已有上千年的历史。骡车，顾名思义就是用骡子拉的车。逢年过节时渭南各地的群众都会相邀数挂骡车前来助兴。骡车大都是由胶轮车或木轱辘车和四匹骡子组成，每匹骡子都系有铜铃，头挂彩饰，背上还插有五面彩色小旗。每辆骡车都有4个吆车和6个敲锣鼓的车夫，他们身着鲜艳的民族服装。每支骡车队都有自己的一套

Driving mule carts is a form of *Shehuo* performance and practiced in Weinan City, Shaanxi Province. Its history stretches back thousands of years. A mule cart, as the name implies, is a cart pulled by a mule. At festivals or several days before and after New Year's Day, people from different parts of Weinan City will drive, at the organiser's invitation, a number of mule carts for entertainment. A mule cart is usually either a rubber-wheeled cart or a wooden cart pulled by four mules. Each mule has a copper bell tethered to it, and is decorated with coloured ornaments on its head, and five coloured flags along its back. Each mule cart is equipped with four muleteers and six farmer artists to hit gongs and beat drums, who are dressed in brightly-coloured national costumes. Each mule cart team has its

鼓谱，称为鼓歌。鼓歌是一支骡车队无形的旗帜和标识，一来营造欢乐气氛，二来以锣鼓驱邪。跑骡车时吆骡人把鞭子一甩，骡子即开始狂奔，同时锣鼓声、铜铃声和成千上万观众的呐喊声、喝彩声响成一片。这时既是骡车表演的亮点，也是最能吸引观众眼球的看点。

own set of drum scores, called Drum Songs. A Drum Song is an invisible flag and insignia of a mule cart team, which on the one hand creates a festival and joyful atmosphere and on the other hand wards off evil spirits with gongs and drums. When driving a mule cart, the muleteer cracks his or her whip, and the mule starts to gallop wildly. At the same time, the sound of gongs and drums, copper bells, and the shouts and cheers of thousands of spectators ring out. This race is not only the highlight of the mule cart show, but also the most eye-catching moment for the audience.

Pic. 23　Driving a Mule Cart Illustrated by Mathew Russell

骡子属马和驴的杂交代，其灵性、爆发力、耐力、免疫力等方面都显现出一定的优势。跑骡车是当地群众自娱自乐的一种文化活动，作为渭南民间社火的独特形式流传下来，有着较高的历史价值、文化价值、艺术价值和社会价值。它既体现了秦人粗犷、豪迈、豁达、乐观的性格，又有增强团结、互助友爱、凝聚人心的作用，寄托了人们对生活的热爱和对美好未来的向往与追求。跑骡车已列入陕西省第二批非物质文化遗产名录。

The mule is a hybrid of the horse and the donkey, bearing such species features as spirituality, explosive power, endurance, and immunity. Driving mule carts is a cultural activity with which local people entertain themselves. It has been passed down as a unique form of folk *Shehuo* performance in Weinan City. It has high historical, cultural, artistic, and social value. It not only embodies the straightforward, heroic, open-minded and optimistic character of the local people, but also enhances solidarity, mutual assistance and friendship, and cohesion. It embodies people's love for life and pursuit of a hopeful future. Driving Mule Carts was listed among the second batch of the Intangible Cultural Heritage in Shaanxi Province.

2.11 华阴司家秋千会
The Sijia Swing Fair in Huayin City

陕西省华阴市司家秋千会是一种独具特色的民俗活动。司家秋千活动的勃兴受

The Sijia Swing Fair in Huayin City, Shaanxi Province is a folk custom activity with distinct local charisma. This activity arose and flourished thanks to the influence of martial

军旅文化影响。相传该村是清朝时扼守潼关军事要塞的一处驻军营地,有个姓胡的军官受到司家清明节秋千活动的启发,就在场地上架了多个秋千,让士兵们以荡秋千为乐。后来,这批军人由屯田而转化为当地的村民,每年清明节他们都要举办一

culture. Legend has it that the village was once a garrison camp stationed to guard Tongguan, a strategic military fortress in the Qing Dynasty. An army officer with the surname Hu was inspired by the Sijia swing activity on Qingming Festival, so he set up a number of swings on the ground, allowing the soldiers to enjoy playing on them. Later, these soldiers were demobbed and settled down as local villagers. Every year during the Qingming Festival, they held a large-scale Swing Fair, and the types of swinging activities grew in

Pic. 24　Swing Fair Illustrated by Mathew Russell

次较大规模的秋千会，秋千活动的品类也日益丰富，竞技性也越来越高。长此以往就逐渐演变为固定的古会，成为这一带农村文化生活的亮点。

司家秋千种类较多，最兴盛时发展到10多种，现保存下来的有架子秋千、地轮子秋千、牌楼秋千、线轮秋千等。司家秋千多姿多彩，妙趣横生，既有体育竞技特点，也有独特的民俗特点，是一项兼具健身和娱乐功能的民俗活动。华阴司家秋千会已列入陕西省第二批非物质文化遗产名录。

abundance and became more and more competitive. Over time, this gradually evolved into a fixed ancient fair and became a highlight of cultural life in this rural area.

There were many kinds of Sijia swings—more than a dozen in fact at the peak of its prosperity. At present one can still observe *Jiazi* swing (a seat hanging by two ropes or chains from a metal or wooden frame), *Dilunzi* swing (two swing seats hang alongside each other from a metal or wooden beam), *Pailou* swing (two seats hanging from the beam of a *pailou*, or decorated memorial archway), and wire wheel swing, to name just several. The Sijia swing is vivid and interesting. It bears the characteristics of being a sports competition while forming a unique folk custom. It is a popular activity that can both entertain people and encourage fitness. The Sijia Swing Fair in Huayin City was listed among the second batch of the Intangible Cultural Heritage in Shaanxi Province.

2.12 蕴空山庙会
The Mount Yunkong Temple Fair

蕴空山禅院位于陕西省渭南市华县大明镇里峪口村南的蕴空山上,每年农历三月十七日这里都会举办蕴空山庙会。蕴空山庙会历史悠久。据考证,从东汉起就有此习俗,距今已有1 900多年的历史。每逢庙会期间,方圆几百里的人们都会起早参加庙会。寺院内游人如织,击缶诵经,祭拜祈福,香烟缭绕,锣鼓喧天,鞭炮齐鸣,热闹非凡。

蕴空山庙会的主要内容一个是群众性集体庙祭求福活动。参加庙会的群众或在大雄宝殿念经、叩头、烧香,或在药王洞求药

The Mount Yunkong Buddhist Temple is located on Mount Yunkong, south of Liyukou Village, Daming Town, Hua County, Weinan City, Shaanxi Province. The Mount Yunkong Buddhist Temple Fair is held here on the 17th day of the lunar March every year. Research has revealed that the event has a long history stretching back more than 1,900 years. It can be traced back to the Eastern Han Dynasty (25–220). During the temple fair, people from within a radius of hundreds of miles will rise early to participate. The Buddhist temple hustles and bustles with crowds of visitors striking the *fou* (an ancient percussion instrument made of clay) to chant scriptures, worshipping and praying for blessings. The temple is wreathed in incense smoke and there is the deafening peal of gongs and drums, creating an extraordinarily boisterous scene.

The main content of the Mount Yunkong Temple Fair encompasses mass collective temple worship and activities for praying for blessings. The participants either chant scriptures, kowtow, burn incense in the Great Buddha Hall, or pray in the King of Medicine Cave for

免除病魔，或在送子娘娘洞祈求赐子。另一个内容是群众瞻仰观光及思想、经济、文化活动。香客们要到南殿数罗汉，要游览观赏三塔（汉塔、宋塔、清塔），要瞻仰历史奇迹悬棺，还要在关公祠祭拜英烈，学习英烈为国为民效忠的精神。

庙会期间也进行物资交流和举办社火、秧歌、皮影、自乐班、杂耍、锣鼓表演、图

relief from illness. Alternatively, they might pray for a baby in the Cave of Songzi Niangniang, a Taoist fertility goddess who is believed to help bring forth children. The event also includes sightseeing and other activities with ideological, economic and cultural contents. Pilgrims will go to the South Hall to count the numbers of arhat or arahant,① visit the Three Pagodas (one from the Han Dynasty, one from the Song Dynasty and one from the Qing Dynasty), pay homage to the historical miracle that is the hanging coffins. People also visit the Guan Yu② Temple to worship the great hero for his allegiance to his country and his people as well.

The temple fair has its dynamic spectacles, as well, such as *Shehuo* performances, *yangge* dance, shadow play, local self-entertaining opera performances, juggling, gong and drum

---

① In Buddhism, an arhat or arahant is one who has gained insight into the true nature of existence and has achieved nirvana. Mahayana Buddhist traditions have used the term for people far advanced along the path of Enlightenment, but who may not have reached full Buddhahood.

② Guan Yu was a Chinese military general serving under the warlord Liu Bei during the late Eastern Han Dynasty of China. Along with Zhang Fei, he shared a brotherly relationship with Liu Bei and accompanied him on most of his early exploits. Guan Yu played a significant role in the events leading up to the end of the Han Dynasty and the establishment of Liu Bei's state of Shu Han during the Three Kingdoms Period (220-280).

书销售等活动。蕴空山庙会的宗旨是合会共议，民主自由，一秉虔心，公议助善，自办庙会，体现了民间群众极强的组织协调能力。蕴空山庙会保留了华县周边地区以民间信仰为特点的传统民间文化，是研究关中东部地区民俗文化的重要依据。蕴空山庙会已列入陕西省第二批非物质文化遗产名录。

performances, book sales and so on. The activity aims to promote the collective governance of local affairs under the rule of democracy, freedom, devotion, and charity. The self-sponsored temple fair thereby reflects the strong organisational and co-ordinating abilities of the people. The Mount Yunkong Temple Fair preserves the traditional culture of Hua County and its surroundings, characterised by folk beliefs. It forms an important basis for the study of the folk culture in the eastern part of the Guanzhong Plain. The Mount Yunkong Temple Fair was listed among the second batch of the Intangible Cultural Heritage in Shaanxi Province.

2.13 医陶始祖与雷公庙会

The Sage of Ceramics and Pharmacology and Leigong Temple Fair

陕西省渭南市白水县是陶圣雷公的故里。据《白水县志》载："雷公，名祥，大雷公村人，曾任'处方''陶王'，黄帝授以《内外经》。"千百年来，乡民把雷祥奉

Baishui County in Weinan City, Shaanxi Province was the hometown of Leigong, the Sage of Ceramics. According to the *Annals of Baishui County* (*Bai shui xian zhi*), "Leigong, whose given name was Xiang, was a native of Grand Leigong Village. He once served during the reign of the Yellow Emperor as a *Chufang* (literally prescription-giving medical official) and Sage of

为"陶圣","雷公造碗"的故事广为流传。陶瓷行业尊其为"开山之祖",依"一日之师,终身为父"之行规民俗,故又称其为"亚父",将其所造陶瓷称为"雷公器"。人们为纪念这位"陶艺之神",在其家乡陵墓前建"雷公庙"。清代《白水县志》载:该庙"创建年代无考,元至正十二年(1352)重修,乡民岁十月二十二日祀"。该庙会兴盛于元,延续于明清民国时期,每逢庙会,赴会者多达数万人。抗日战争后庙会衰落。

Ceramics, and was instructed by the Yellow Emperor with his research on *The Internal and External Canon*." For thousands of years, village people have regarded him as the Sage of Ceramics, and the story of "Leigong creating a bowl" is widespread among people. He was honoured and respected by the ceramics industry as "the ancestor of pottery" and was also hailed as "God Father" according to the folk custom that stipulates one always respect your teacher as you do your father. The ceramic products of his therefore are called "Leigong wares". The Leigong Temple was built in front of his mausoleum in his hometown to commemorate this Sage of Ceramics. The *Annals of Baishui County* in the Qing Dynasty record that "the date when the Leigong Temple was built is not verified. But what is certain is that the temple was rebuilt in the 12th year of the Zhizheng Period (1341-1370) of the Yuan Dynasty in 1352, and the villagers worshipped here on the 22nd day of the lunar October. The temple fair thrived in the Yuan Dynasty and endured during the Ming and Qing Dynasties and the Republic of China. During the temple fair days, tens of thousands of people would attend the temple fair, though it fell into decline after the Anti-Japanese War (1931-1945).

医陶始祖与雷公庙会是以民间信仰为主要内容的民间群众性文化活动，也是古时民间陶瓷商贸集会。这一活动见于陕西省白水县城东南8公里的冯雷镇大雷公村。每年农历四月二十二日和十月二十二日，香客、乡民、郎中及陶瓷艺人、窑主均云集于此，他们先在雷公庙和雷公墓地烧香焚表祭神，再到"亚父行宫"祭拜，求医祈福，此后进行陶瓷成品交易，至晚在戏楼前观戏，一连数日。再现医陶始祖与雷公庙会对于传承我国陶瓷文化，推崇中华民族尊祖敬贤美德具有重要意义。医陶始祖与雷公庙会已列入陕西省第二批非物质文化遗产名录。

The Temple Fair is a popular folk cultural activity with folk beliefs as the main content. It also happens to be an ancient folk ceramics trade fair held within Grand Leigong Village in Fenglei Town, 8 kilometres southeast of the county town in Baishui County, Shaanxi Province. Every year on the 22nd April and 22nd October according to the Lunar Calendar, pilgrims, villagers, herbalists, ceramic artists, and kiln masters gather here. First of all, they burn incense and pen vows to worship at the Grand Leigong Temple and the Leigong Burial Ground, and then they worship at "God Father's Palace", seeking after medical treatment and praying for blessings. Afterwards, they trade ceramic products and watch operas in front of the opera house for several days in a row. The revival of this temple fair is of great significance to ensuring the survival of China's ceramic culture and advocating the Chinese nation's virtues of respecting ancestors and virtuous individuals. The Leigong Temple Fair was listed among the second batch of the Intangible Cultural Heritage in Shaanxi Province.

2.14 香山庙会
The Fragrant Mountain Temple Fair

香山寺位于陕西省铜川市耀州区西北部，香山寺古刹是我国四大香山之一，也是我国八大佛教圣地之一。据史料记载，香山寺院始建于符秦（351—394），至隋唐时即成为佛教圣地。每逢庙会时，朝山的佛门僧侣、善男信女纷至沓来、络绎不绝。香山传统庙会分别在每年农历三月初五至十五和十月初五至十五举办春季和秋季庙会各一次，以春季庙会为最盛。香山庙会是以民间信仰为主要内容的民间群众性活动。正会前即有香客居士、僧众自四方翩然而至，求佛护佑、祈福禳灾、求子祛病、求平安顺当等。庙会期间，寺

The Fragrant Mountain Temple is located in the northwest of Yaozhou District in Tongchuan City, Shaanxi Province. The Fragrant Mountain Temple is one of the four major fragrant mountains in China and one of the eight major Buddhist holy lands in the country as well. According to historical records, the Fragrant Mountain Temple was built during the Former Qin period (351−394), and developed into a Buddhist holy site in the Sui and Tang Dynasties (581−907). At temple fairs, Buddhist monks, philanthropists, and devout men and women flock to the mountain in an endless stream. The traditional spring and autumn temple fairs are held respectively from the 5th to the 15th days of March and the 5th to the 15th days of October according to the Lunar Calendar, with the spring temple fair being the most prosperous. This temple fair held at the Fragrant Mountain Temple is a mass folk activity with folk beliefs as its mainstay. Before the temple fair starts, pilgrims and monks come from all directions to pray for the Buddha's protection, blessings, baby bestowing, relief from illness, and for safety and prosperity.

院规定：十方僧俗朝山拜佛，皆以诚敬待之，不得攀附权势，厚此薄彼。初六至十五为正会，初一至初五为准备阶段，打扫卫生，清整环境，接待香客，安排住宿。昔日由于交通不便，远道而来者，被安排在城里香山下院的广福庵、广严寺和山寿寺内，后择吉上山。这些香客除本地拜佛者外，尚有外埠及港澳同胞。

香山庙会期间，寺院日日都需拜佛、上供、焚香、焚表、诵经、免费开斋饭，循序进行，有条不紊。初六至十五正会进行期间，人头攒动，香烟缭绕，许愿还愿，络

During the temple fair, the temple stipulates that monks and lay people from all directions coming to the mountain to worship god should be treated with sincerity and respect. Showing special favour to those of high status is strictly forbidden. The 6th to the 15th days of the lunar month are set aside for the regular meeting, and the 1st to the 5th days are the preparation stage, which includes cleaning the environment, receiving pilgrims and arranging accommodation. In the past, due to the inconvenience of transportation, those who came from afar arranged to live temporarily in the Guangfu Nunnery, the Guangyan Temple, and the Shanshou Temple in the lower courtyard of the Fragrant Mountain in the city, and would climb up the mountain to the temple on an auspicious day. Nowadays, some pilgrims are local worshippers, some from out of town, and others compatriots from Hong Kong and Macao.

During the temple fair, people worship the Buddha, offer up sacrifices, burn incense and written vows, chant scriptures and prepare free vegetarian food every day. All of this is conducted systematically and in an orderly way. From the 6th to the 15th day of the lunar month the regular fair is held. The temple is wreathed in incense smoke with an endless

2 陕西省第二批非物质文化遗产名录中的民俗
The Folk Culture in the Second Batch of the Intangible Cultural Heritage in Shaanxi Province

Pic. 25　Fragrant Mountain Illustrated by Mathew Russell

绎不绝。到了十五这一天,更是香客如云,殿内拥挤不堪。香山庙会保留了铜川市耀州区及其周边地区以民间信仰为特点的传统民间文化,是研究关中地区民众生活和理想信念的重要依据。香山庙会已列入陕西省第二批非物质文化遗产名录。

throng of pilgrims who make or redeem vows. On the 15th day, more pilgrims gather in the fair, forming crowds so huge that the hall overflows. The Fragrant Mountain Temple Fair retains the traditional folk culture of Yaozhou District in Tongchuan City and its surroundings. This is characterised by its folk beliefs, serving as important evidence for further studying the lives, ideals and beliefs of people living with the passes. The Fragrant Mountain Temple Fair was listed among the second batch of the Intangible Cultural Heritage in Shaanxi Province.

2.15 安塞转九曲

Walking the Nine-Twist Maze of Lanterns in Ansai County

陕西省延安市安塞县（今安塞区）的转九曲是当地独具特色的民俗活动形式，主要分布在安塞县境内各大寺庙和乡村中。安塞转九曲俗称"观灯"，一般在特定节庆期间的晚上进行表演。据说转九曲可以给百姓带来吉祥平安，消灾免难，永保太平。因此这项活动深受当地

Walking the Nine-Twist Maze of Lanterns in Ansai County (present-day Ansai District), Yan'an City, Shaanxi Province is a unique form of local folk activity which is mainly distributed among major temples and villages in Ansai County. It is commonly known as "lantern watching", and usually takes place on the evenings of certain festivals. It is believed that the activities can help to bring people good luck, safety and lifelong peace by warding off troubles and disasters, therefore they enjoy great popularity among the local people. The a

**Pic. 26　Walking the Nine-Twist Maze of Lanterns in Ansai County
Illustrated by Mathew Russell**

群众喜爱。安塞转九曲有着文学、音乐、舞蹈、美术、宗教、民俗等文化内涵，基本内容包括诵经、祈祷、偷灯、抢灯、送灯、出场、秧歌腰鼓表演等。在转九曲表演中，需要的器具有中心灯、九曲灯、九曲门等。安塞转九曲的表演时间一般是两小时，转九曲在表演时，人们都陶醉在欢乐喜庆之中。

安塞转九曲凝聚着社会和民众的心理情愫，为活跃群众文化生活注入了新的活力，同时也是研究当地民俗文化的活态资料。由于现代多元文化的冲击，目前参加转九曲的人和举办转九曲活动的村庄越来越少，安塞转九曲这一传统民俗活动面临着消亡的危险，亟待保护。安塞转九曲已列入陕西省第二批非物质文化遗产名录。

ctivities cover cultural connotations, such as literature, music, dances, fine arts, religion and folk customs. The basic content of the activities include chanting scriptures, praying for blessings, stealing lanterns, grabbing lanterns, offering lanterns, stepping on stages, *yangge* dance and waist drum performance, etc. The required instruments include a central lantern, a Jiuqu lantern, a Jiuqu door and so on. The performance generally lasts for two hours in duration. When the activities are being performed, people are intoxicated with joy and happiness.

Walking the Nine-Twist Maze of Lanterns in Ansai County embody the psychological feelings of society and the public, and it functions like injections of new vitality to enliven the cultural life of the masses. Meanwhile, it is also a living repository for studying local folk culture. Owing to the impact of pluralism in modern society, fewer and fewer people and villages participate in and organise the activities. This folk activity faces the danger of disappearance and requires urgent protection. Walking the Nine-Twist Maze of Lanterns in Ansai County was listed among the second batch of the Intangible Cultural Heritage in Shaanxi Province.

Pic. 27 The Ansai Waist-Drum Dance Illustrated by Mathew Russell

2.16 横山牛王会
The Niuwang Fair in Hengshan County

陕西省榆林市横山县（今衡山区）的牛王会是当地春节期间的一种大型综合性庙会形式，主要流布于该县无定河两岸41个自然村。其特点是在敬奉老佛爷的同时敬奉一个叫牛王菩萨的神灵。牛王会的正式会期为每年正月十三、十四、十五，共三天。会前从正月初八起，主办村全村开

The Niuwang Fair in Hengshan County (present-day Hengshan District), Yulin City, Shaanxi Province is a large-scale comprehensive temple fair held during the local Spring Festival. It is mainly distributed among 41 villages on the both sides of the River Wuding in the county. Its core activity entails revering the Niuwang Bodhisattva and Laofoye, commonly known as the Buddha. The official time of this fair lasts for three days, covering the 13th, 14th, and 15th days of the first month in Lunar Calendar every year. Before the fair commences, from the 8th day of the first lunar month, the whole population of the host village begins to refrain

始忌口（不食荤腥）并做准备工作，所有准备工作及敬神仪式女性均不参与。正月十三清早，老佛爷和牛王菩萨分乘两座楼轿从华严寺出发被抬往主办村。楼轿所过之处，沿途百姓自愿在路边跪拜，烧香烧纸，放鞭炮，向楼轿磕头，楼轿也向群众回礼，互动场面十分热闹。牛王菩萨到达主办村后被安放在专门为之搭建的临时佛堂。随后三天乡民们为牛王菩萨上香膜拜，轮番上贡，念经，唱戏。

牛王会从正月十三开始上贡，三天三堂贡，名曰"蒸贡""高贡""水贡"。每堂贡有100多碟，分装在48个红色木盘内，由48名男性村民顶在头上，跪成长长两行，在念经声中依次递入佛

from eating meat and fish, and starts to make preparations. Women are forbidden from taking part in all preparations and worship ceremonies. On the early morning of the 13th day of the first lunar month, both the Laofoye and Niuwang Bodhisattva leave the Huayan Temple respectively in two sedan chairs heading for the host village. Wherever the sedan chairs pass, people voluntarily bow down along the roadside, burning incense and ancestor money, setting off firecrackers and kowtowing to the sedan chairs. Then the sedan chairs also return salutes to the crowds. The interaction between them proves very lively. After Niuwang Bodhisattva arrives in the host village, he is placed in a temporary shrine custom-built for him. Over the following three days, villagers will take turns to offer incense, pay tributes, chant scriptures, and sing opera arias.

During the Niuwang Fair, people begin to pay tribute from the 13th day of the first lunar month. Three tributes named the "steamed tribute" (*zheng gong*), the "high tribute" (*gao gong*), and the "water tribute" (*shui gong*) will be given three times in three days. Each tribute is composed of more than one hundred dishes packed onto 48 red wooden plates, carried by 48 male villagers on their heads. They kneel

Pic. 28　Niuwang Fair Illustrated by Mathew Russell

堂。正月十五下午贡上 10 件宝物后结束上贡。会毕，贡品分给主办会的村子的村民。牛王会的念经、迎幡、推幡、升大塔等活动，为的是超度亡灵，禳灾祛疫，除污秽之气。牛王会涉及多方面民间习俗，具有一定的社会文化研究价值。横山牛王会已列入陕西省第二批非物质文化遗产名录。

down onto the ground in two rows and pass wooden plates from one to another into the Buddhist hall to the sound of scriptures being chanted. On the afternoon of the 15th day of the first lunar month, the tribute-offering ceremony ends after 10 treasures have been presented. After the fair, all the tributes will be distributed among the residents of the host village. All the activities, during the fair, such as chanting scriptures, welcoming and pushing-down the ceremonial banner (*fan*), as well as lifting paper towers are meant to release souls from purgatory, ward off disasters and expel evil spirits. The Niuwang Fair involves many

2.17 南郑协税社火高跷
The Xieshui Stilt-Walking *Shehuo* Performance in Nanzheng County

南郑协税社火高跷主要分布在陕西省汉中市南郑县城乡。南郑协税社火高跷历史悠久，在民间有"兴于唐，广于宋，盛于明清"之说。

南郑协税社火高跷脱胎于古代先民祭祀活动中的神戏，从初期单一的宗教祭祀活动逐渐发展演变成为大型民间文化活动形式。南郑协税社火高跷可表演各类历史剧目中的故事，目前保存的折子戏本有180

aspects of folk customs, and is of definite value to social and cultural research. The Niuwang Fair in Hengshan County was listed among the second batch of the Intangible Cultural Heritage in Shaanxi Province.

The Xieshui stilt-walking *Shehuo* performance in Nanzheng County is mainly distributed across the territory of Nanzheng in Hanzhong City, Shaanxi Province. It enjoys a long history and locals believe that "it rose in the Tang Dynasty (618–907), became popular in the Song (960–1279), and flourished in the Ming (1368–1644) and Qing (1636–1912)".

The Xieshui stilt-walking *Shehuo* performance in Nanzheng County grew out of ancient sacred opera accompanying sacrificial activities, and gradually evolved from a pure religious sacrificial activity into a large-scale folk cultural event. The Xieshui stilt-walking *Shehuo* performance in Nanzheng County incorporates various components based upon Chinese historical stories. At present, more than 180 excerpts and scripts have been preserved,

多个，主要剧目有《天荡山》《取经》《打銮驾》《串龙珠》等。

南郑协税社火高跷又叫踩腿子，即在表演时将1.6米至2米长的木质高腿牢固地绑扎在表演者的腿上。表演者身穿古典戏剧服装，手拿道具，在铿锵的锣鼓声中沿街表演。表演者在表演中可前进，可倒退，可跳跃，可左右摇摆，可嬉戏打闹，表演动作惊险奇特，难度较高。南郑协税社火高跷的传统脸型谱式分对脸、破脸、悬脸、碎脸、转脸、定脸六种。南郑协税社火高跷以高、巧、奇、险、美、趣、斗为人称道，深受广大群众喜爱。南郑协税社火高跷已列入陕西省第二批非物质文

including *Mount Tiandang* (*Tian dang shan*), *A Pilgrimage for Buddhist Scriptures* (*Qu jing*), *Beating the Imperial Chariot* (*Da luan jia*), and *Bunching-up Dragon Pearls* (*Chuan long zhu*), to name just a few.

The Xieshui stilt-walking *Shehuo* performance in Nanzheng County is also known as stepping on legs. This refers to the 1.6 to 2-metre long wooden stilts which are tied firmly to the performer's legs during the display. The performers wear classical theatrical costumes, hold props, and perform along the streets to the sound of sonorous drums and gongs. The performers can move forward, back up, jump, swing to the left and right, and interact with each other. The performances are extremely thrilling to watch but hard to accomplish. Traditional facial make-up during the stilt-walking is divided into six types: symmetrical faces, asymmetrical fierce faces, faces for fierce images, faces with wrinkles, substitutable faces, and faces with fixed features. The Xieshui stilt-walking *Shehuo* performance has been acclaimed for its great stature, ingenuity, strangeness, riskiness, beauty, fun, and fighting, and is a firm favourite with the people. The Xieshui Stilt-Walking *Shehuo* Performance in Nanzheng County was listed among the second batch of

2.18 谷雨公祭仓颉仪式

The Grain-Rain Day Official Worship Ceremony for Cang Jie

谷雨公祭仓颉仪式流传于陕西省商洛市洛南县境内。早在公元前2800年左右,黄帝史官仓颉在洛河旁受"元扈凤图""阳虚鸟迹"的启示,创造了惊天地、泣鬼神的鸟迹图形字符,并将其中二十八字手书刻于元扈山峭壁之上,开创了人类文明的先河。洛南人民为了纪念造字始祖,传承民族文明,便于每年谷雨之时举行祭祀书圣仓颉活动。

洛南谷雨祭祀仓颉仪式,大约在春秋时期就已有之。起初以民祭为主,由地方

The Grain-Rain Day Official Worship Ceremony for Cang Jie is to be found in Luonan County, Shangluo City, Shaanxi Province. As early as around 2,800 BC, the Yellow Emperor employed a historiographer named Cang Jie. During his trip to Luonan County, Cang Jie was inspired by the birds' footprints in Mount Yuanhu and Mount Yangxu alongside the River Luo, and duly created 28 bird-shaped characters that startled the universe and moved the gods. He carved those characters onto the cliff at Mount Yuanhu, marking the advent of human civilisation. In order to commemorate the inventor of Chinese characters and transmit national civilisation, the people of Luonan hold a worship ceremony for Cang Jie on every Grain-Rain Day.

The worship ceremony can be dated back to around the time of the Spring and Autumn Period. Back then, it mainly took the form of local sacrifices arranged by local organisations.

团体出面组织，区域涉及洛南、商州、蓝田、渭南、华阴等方圆几百里之地。每年谷雨时，香客们手持香表，提着供品，从四乡八里来到许庙，祭拜上供。供品多以面食蒸制而成，盘花中鸟虫鱼，栩栩如生，这种形式已延续几千年。清光绪三年（1877），洛南县令伊允桢于县城东街仓圣祠首开谷雨公祭仓颉典礼。从此，祭祀活动由民祭上升为官祭，不仅规模扩大，规格提高，而且形成了一整套祭祀程序。此后历任县令均有公祭。2001年，洛南县政府在县城首办仓颉文化艺术节。2008年谷雨前夕，洛南县政府又在县城南坡新建仓颉园，并举行了隆重的公祭仪式，将这一民俗文化活动推

The regions involved include Luonan, Shangzhou, Lantian, Weinan, Huayin and other places across a radius of hundreds of miles. On every Grain-Rain Day, pilgrims come to the Xu Temple from all directions, with incense, written wishes of blessings, and offerings for worship and tribute. Most of the offerings consist of steamed dough models. These include convincing likenesses of flowers, birds, insects and fish. This tradition has lasted for thousands of years. In the third year (1877) of the reign of the Emperor Guangxu of Qing, Yi Yunzhen, the Magistrate of Luonan County, initiated the Cang Jie worship ceremony on Grain-Rain Day at the ancestral temple for Cangjie, named the Cangsheng Temple on the east street of the county town. Since then, this activity has been upgraded from a local sacrifice to an official one, and has been expanded in scale and status, as well as being formalised with a complete set of sacrificial procedures. Successive county magistrates have upheld this ritual. In 2001, the County Government of Luonan held the first Cang Jie Culture and Art Festival. On the eve of Grain-Rain Day in 2008, the local authority built a new Cang Jie Park on the southern slope of the county and held a grand public memorial ceremony, thus pushing this folk cultural activity

向了一个新的高度。

仓颉造字在中国历史文化中占有重要地位。其深刻的文化内涵和历史底蕴越来越引起国内外华人和专家学者的关注。谷雨公祭仓颉仪式这一民俗形式，有效继承、弘扬和传播了中华汉字文明这一主题文化，激励人民群众发扬先祖精神，不断追求社会进步。谷雨公祭仓颉仪式已列入陕西省第二批非物质文化遗产名录。

to a new height.

Cang Jie creating characters played an important role in Chinese history and culture. Its cultural connotations and historical profundity have attracted more and more attention from Chinese people together with that from experts and scholars at home and abroad. The ceremony inherits, promotes and spreads in an effective way the civilisation of Chinese characters. It also inspires the Chinese people to carry forward the spirit of their ancestors for the continuous pursuit of social progress. The Grain-Rain Day Official Worship Ceremony for Cang Jie was listed among the second batch of the Intangible Cultural Heritage in Shaanxi Province.

2.19 丹凤高台芯子

The *Shehuo* Performance on High Platform *Xinzi* in Danfeng County

陕西省商洛市丹凤县的高台芯子属于民间社火形式之一。它起源于宋元时期，世代相传，生生不息。

The *Shehuo* performance on high platform *Xinzi* in Danfeng County, Shangluo City, Shaanxi Province is a form of acrobatic and pyrotechnic performance. It originated in the Song (960–1279) and Yuan (1271–1368) Dynasties and has been passed down from

丹凤高台芯子既表现了秦人的勇敢豪放，又体现了江南楚文化的委婉细腻，形成了独特的艺术风格。它的制作需要芯桩、抬杠、麻绳、芯杆等材

generation to generation.

　　The *Shehuo* on high platform *Xinzi* in Danfeng County not only manifests the bravery and boldness of people in the land of Qin, but also reflects the mild and meticulous characteristics of the Chu culture prevalent in southern China, forming a unique artistic style. The production requires stakes, beams, hemp

Pic. 29　Military *Xinzi* Illustrated by Mathew Russell

料，其中芯杆是丹凤高台芯子制作中最主要的部分。艺人们运用力学原理，根据造型要求将精心设计好的芯杆固定在方桌上，用作装扮各类造型的型号。然后把化好妆，穿上戏服的小孩绑上去，一台芯子就装扮完成了。丹凤高台芯子分为文芯子、武芯子、血芯子三大类。文芯子以表演爱情故事为主；武芯子以刀枪、棍棒为道具，以武打造型为主，借以弘扬正气，惩恶扬善；血芯子以渲染恐怖气氛见长，令人胆战心惊。丹凤高台芯子有独芯子、双芯子、众芯子、转芯子、吊芯子、背芯子、担芯子等形式。丹凤高台芯子与当地群众的生活习俗密切相关，每逢重大节日，丹凤人都要表演高台

ropes, poles and other materials. Among these, the pole is the most important part. Artists apply mechanical principles to fix well-designed poles onto a square table to be a core part of a *Xinzi*, according to the modelling requirements. When children made up and dressed in costumes are tied up onto those poles, the making and decoration of a *Xinzi* is thus completed. The *Shehuo* on high platform *Xinzi* in the Danfeng County are divided into three categories：Civil *Xinzi*, Military *Xinzi* and Bloody *Xinzi*. Civil *Xinzi* performance tells mainly love stories; Military *Xinzi* uses blades, spears, and sticks as props to make various fighting poses, by which it encourages righteousness and kindness; Bloody *Xinzi* is known for creating a grand thrilling atmosphere, which is terrifying. In terms of forms, the *Shehuo* performance on high platform *Xinzi* includes Single *Xinzi*, Double *Xinzi*, Multiple *Xinzi*, Revolving *Xinzi*, Hanging *Xinzi*, Balancing *Xinzi*, Shouldering *Xinzi* and so on. The *Shehuo* performance on high platform *Xinzi* is closely related to the living customs of local people. During major festivals, Danfeng residents will perform the *Xinzi* to enhance the liveliness of the atmosphere. The *Shehuo* Performance on High Platform *Xinzi* in Danfeng County was

芯子以增加节日的热烈气氛。丹凤高台芯子已列入陕西省第二批非物质文化遗产名录。

listed among the second batch of the Intangible Cultural Heritage in Shaanxi Province.

3 陕西省第三批
非物质文化遗产名录中的民俗

The Folk Culture in the
Third Batch of the Intangible Cultural
Heritage in Shaanxi Province

3.1 上巳节风俗
The Customs of Shangsi Festival

上巳节风俗主要流传于西安市。上巳节为三月上旬的巳月，曹魏之后定为三月初三。上巳节最早可以追溯到春秋时期。据传，三月上巳这一天，郑国男女到溱、洧二水岸边举行祭祀，消除灾害。少男少女们也借此春游的机会谈情说爱。《诗经》中《溱洧》一诗对这一民间风俗的盛况有生动的描写。秦汉以来，上巳节更是

Shangsi Festival customs are to be found throughout Xi'an City. The festival originally took place during the first ten days of the Lunar March. After the Cao-Wei[①] regime (220−266), it was designated to take place on the 3rd day of the lunar March. The Shangsi Festival can be traced back to the Spring and Autumn Period (770 BC−476 BC). Legend has it that on the 3rd day of the third lunar month, men and women in the State of Zheng held sacrifices on the banks of the Rivers Zhen and Wei to ward off disasters. Boys and girls also took this as a chance to seek romance. In the *Book of Songs* (*Shi jing*), a poem titled *The Zhen and Wei*[②] gives a vivid description of the pomp of this folk custom. Since the Qin and

---

① Cao-Wei was one of the three major states that competed for supremacy over China in the Three Kingdoms Period. The state was established by Cao Pi in 220, based upon the foundations laid by his father, Cao Cao, towards the end of the Eastern Han Dynasty. The name "Wei" first became associated with Cao Cao when he was named the Duke of Wei by the Eastern Han government in 213, and became the name of the state when Cao Pi proclaimed himself emperor in 220. Historians often add the prefix "Cao" to distinguish it from other Chinese states known as "Wei", such as Wei of the Warring States period and Northern Wei of the Northern and Southern Dynasties.

② Zhen and Wei are major rivers in the state of Zheng, tributaries to the Yellow River. Zheng was a powerful state located south of the Yellow River in present-day western Henan and was an important ally of the Eastern Zhou court.

发展成为全国性的大节日。据《汉书·礼仪志》记载:"是月上巳,官民皆洁于东流水上,曰洗濯祓除,去宿垢疢(病)为大洁。"到了晋代,始有曲水流觞之饮。《荆楚岁时记》记载:"三月三日,士民并出江渚池沼间,为流觞曲水之饮。"除

Han Dynasties, Shangsi Festival has developed into a national festival. According to the *Book of Han*: *Annals of Etiquette* (*Han shu li yi zhi*), "In the Lunar March, both officials and ordinary people alike bathe themselves in the eastward flowing water to wash away dirt and diseases, ensuring thorough cleanliness." The Jin Dynasty witnessed the start of the tradition of wine cups floating on a winding canal, namely, to treat friends with banquets and *baijiu*—drinking by waterside. According to the *Records*

Pic. 30　Shangsi Festival Illustrated by Mathew Russell

此以外，还产生了上巳节"曲水浮素卵"或"曲水浮绛枣"的游戏，即将鸡蛋或枣放在水中，漂到谁面前，谁就取食，以此为戏。

of the Land of Jingchu (modern-day Hubei Province) (*Jingchu sui shi ji*[①]), "On the 3rd day of the third lunar month, both officials and ordinary people held banquets by rivers, lakes and ponds to treat friends by drinking *baijiu*." In addition, on the day of Shangsi Festival itself, there were also games like "floating eggs downstream" or "floating dates downstream". That is to say, eggs or dates were placed into the water floating down from the upper reaches of a river. Whoever it stopped in front of was allowed to eat it.

盛唐时，每逢上巳节，皇帝都会携妃子百官游览皇家园林——芙蓉园。长安民众也纷纷前往曲江欢聚游宴。杜甫《丽人行》中"三月三日天气新，长安水边多丽人"就描写了上巳节长安曲江禊饮踏青的盛况。这正是今天西安曲江三月三上巳节民俗活动的来历。

In the Tang Dynasty, the emperor would take his concubines and officials to visit the Royal Hibiscus Garden at Shangsi. The citizens of Chang'an would also head to the River Qujiang for a banquet. Du Fu's poem, *A Beauty's Spring Tour by the Riverside* (*Li ren xing*), relates that "(the) weather is fine on the 3rd March, with many beauties out by the riverside". He was referring to the grand scene on the day of Shangsi Festival when girls and ladies went out for a spring tour by the River Qujiang in Chang'an City. That is the precise origin of the folk custom activities on Shangsi Festival by the River Qujiang in Xi'an City.

[①] It is a description of holidays in central China during the 6th and 7th centuries. It was compiled by Du Gongzhan in the Sui or early Tang as a revised, annotated edition of Zong Lin's *Record of Jingchu* in the middle 6th century.

大唐芙蓉园建于原唐代芙蓉园遗址之上，是中国第一个全方位展示盛唐皇家园林风貌的大型文化主题公园。目前，上巳节活动尚未在全社会范围内得到恢复。但是自 2005 年以来，大唐芙蓉园为挖掘传承上巳节这一盛唐极具代表性的节日做了很大的努力，同时也得到了广大社会民众的积极配合、响应，专家学者的倡导和认可。比如 2007 年，大唐芙蓉园举行了冠礼、袚禊、曲水流觞、踏青抛彩等"三月三·上巳节"相关精彩活动，让公众切身体验上巳古礼；2008 年，大唐芙蓉园举办了上巳踏青文化节，通过丰富多彩的古代游艺活动，如大唐斗鸡、蹴鞠、秋千等，让民众体验古人上巳节踏青游艺之趣。此外，大唐芙

Built on the original site of the Grand Tang Royal Hibiscus Garden, the Grand Tang Hibiscus Garden is the first large-scale cultural theme park of its kind to fully display the grandeur of the royal gardens in the heyday of the Tang Dynasty. At present, the revival of Shangsi Festival activities has not extended to the whole of society. However, since 2005, the Grand Tang Hibiscus Garden has striven to continue the Shangsi Festival tradition, a representative festival of Tang times. The public have co-operated in this enterprise and showed great enthusiasm, whilst experts and scholars have lent their advocacy and recognition, too. In 2007, in the Grand Tang Hibiscus Garden "the 3rd March Shangsi Festival" activities were held to allow the public to experience ancient festive traditions, like the coming-of-age ceremony, bathing by the riverside, and throwing embroidered balls. In 2008, the garden staged a spring-outing cultural festival, with a variety of colourful ancient entertainment activities, such as the Grand Tang cockfighting, *Cuju* (a game similar to football), and swinging to allow the public to experience the interest of the ancient festival. Moreover, when the garden celebrates its opening anniversary every year, it will organise Shangsi Festival-themed activities in that month, making the Shangsi Festival deeply

蓉园每年在庆祝开园周年的同时开展上巳节文化主题月活动,让上巳节深入人心。上巳节风俗已列入陕西省第三批非物质文化遗产名录。

rooted in the hearts of the people. Shangsi Festival customs were listed among the third batch of the Intangible Cultural Heritage in Shaanxi Province.

3.2 终南山钟馗信仰民俗

The Customs for Worshipping Zhong Kui in the Zhongnan Mountains

钟馗是中国民间信仰中唯一一位多角色神祇。他在春节时是门神,端午时是斩五毒的天师,有时在民间还充当文武财神及魁星、石榴花神等角色,寄托着人们对正气、正义和福气的祈愿,是公认的"赐福镇宅圣君"。

Zhong Kui is the only deity in Chinese folk belief to whom multiple functions have been assigned. He serves as the door guardian during Spring Festival and catcher of poisonous insects at Dragon Boat Festival, as well as sometimes being the God of Wealth, the Deity of Examinations (Kui xing[①]), and the Pomegranate God. Zhong Kui has been recognised as "the Holy King to bestow blessings and protect households". Therefore, people petition him for uprightness, righteousness, and good luck.

终南山位于西安市南,是秦岭山脉的一段。而终南山户县一带

Located to the south of Xi'an City, the Zhongnan Mountains are an arm of the Qinling Mountain Range. The area around Hu County in

---

[①]He is the deity of scholars who took imperial examinations. Before the imperial examinations weres discontinued in 1905, virtually every Chinese scholar gave Kui a place of honor in his home, with images and name tablets.

Pic. 31　Zhong Kui Illustrated by Mathew Russell

被认为是钟馗故里，在当地民众生活中演绎出了许多颇有特色的钟馗信仰民俗活动。终南山钟馗信仰民俗主要包括以下三个方面：

一是跳钟馗赛社民俗。这是流传于钟馗故里户县及其周边地区的一种古老的祈福民俗活动，包括跳钟馗赛社大傩仪和跳钟馗小傩仪两种形式。其中跳钟馗赛

the Zhongnan Mountains is considered to be the homeland of Zhong Kui, and there many customs and activities with local characteristics have developed which manifest this belief. The customs mainly cover the following three aspects:

First of all is the Zhong Kui Dance. This is an ancient blessing folk activity distributed around Hu County and surrounding areas of Zhong Kui's hometown. The activity includes two forms of dance: the Major Rite of *Nuo* and Minor Rite of *Nuo* of these. The Major Rite of *Nuo* is solemn and grand in nature, being a mass

社大傩仪活动隆重而又盛大，是群众性的祛邪、祈福盛典。迎神队伍首先要去钟馗庙里迎神，迎神队伍由傩神队和耍龙舞狮及大头娃表演队伍组成，全村群众紧随其后，走街串巷，长达数里，蔚为壮观。跳钟馗小傩仪是为事主家中进行钟馗祈福镇宅的小型傩仪形式。

二是钟馗崇拜及中堂挂像习俗。钟馗虽为民间所推崇，但却少见于各地庙宇，而户县凡寺庙多有钟馗神位，甚至还有钟馗专庙，如石井镇钟馗宫、甘河钟馗庙等；不少村口还立碑刻钟馗画像或钟馗塑像。大王镇一带在结婚时，会专设钟馗神位敬奉，求钟馗保佑，多子多福。其他地方的钟馗画像一般仅限于"钟馗打鬼""钟馗嫁妹"两

ceremony for banishing evil and praying for blessings. The welcoming team will first go to the Zhong Kui Temple to receive the deity Zhong Kui. This group consists of the god-receiving team, the dragon and lion dance team and the big-headed children performing team (young dancers wear huge papier mache heads in the likeness of children). Nearly all villagers follow closely and wander about the streets for several miles, creating a very spectacular scene of its kind. By contrast, the Minor Rite of *Nuo* is a smaller-scale ceremony to pray to the god Zhong Kui for his blessings and to protect the host house.

Second comes worshipping Zhong Kui and hanging his portrait as the central scroll. Although Zhong Kui is worshipped by ordinary folk, his likeness is rarely to be seen in temples in other places. Hu County is an exception. Here one can find the spirit tablet of Zhong Kui in most temples, with some special foundations even being dedicated to him. These include the Zhong Kui Palace in Shijing Town and the Zhong Kui Temple in Ganhe Town. The entrances to many villages are adorned with Zhong Kui's portrait or statues of him. When people in Dawang Town get married, they will set up the spirit tablet of Zhong Kui for his blessings in the form of more children and good fortune. Meanwhile, in other

两种，或作为门神，春节时贴于门上。而户县钟馗画像不仅种类纷繁，多达百余种，而且作为中堂画，悬挂于中堂之上，用于镇宅祈福。其他民间美术形式，剪纸、绘画、皮影、雕塑、麦秆画等也都有表现钟馗题材的作品。

三是钟馗的民间传说丰富。如《钟馗与终南山的传说》《唐玄奘与钟馗的传说》《财神刘海与钟馗的传说》等。

终南山钟馗信仰民俗活动以古老的傩文化为基础，融入了自然崇拜、鬼神崇拜、生殖崇拜等内容，具有重要的历史、文化和学术研究价值。终南山钟馗信仰民俗已列入陕西省第三批非物质文化遗产名录。

places, portraits of Zhong Kui generally depict "Zhong Kui fighting a ghost" or "Zhong Kui sending his sister to be married". Every year before Spring Festival, portraits of Zhong Kui are posted onto gates to be revered as a door god. But the portraits of this deity in Hu County, are not only diverse in nature, with more than one hundred kinds, but he is also treated as the central scroll and hung on the wall of every family's living room to protect that household. Other folk arts forms, such as paper-cutting, painting, shadow puppetry, sculpture and wheat straw painting, are also rich in Zhong Kui-themed motifs.

Third is the abundance of folk tales about Zhong Kui, including *The Legend of Zhong Kui and the Zhongnan Mountains*, *The Legend of Xuanzang of Tang and Zhong Kui*, *The Legend of the God of Wealth Liu Hai and Zhong Kui*, etc.

Based on the ancient Taoist rite of *Nuo*, the customs for worshipping Zhong Kui in the Zhongnan Mountains have appropriated elements of pantheism, worship of ghosts and gods, petitioning for fertility and other contents, which bestow on it important historical, cultural and academic research value. The Customs for Worshipping Zhong Kui in the Zhongnan Mountains were listed among the third batch of the Intangible Cultural Heritage in Shaanxi Province.

3.3 西王禹村纸台

The Paper Platform of Xiwangyu Village

咸阳市礼泉县阡东镇西王禹村的纸台是一种含有历史、宗教、民俗、艺术等诸多文化内容的别具特色的社火艺术形式。关于"纸台社火"的来源,当地有这样的说法:

相传,公元前2000年左右,大禹治水来到

The paper platform of Xiwangyu Village is popular in Qiandong Town, Liquan County, Xianyang City. It is a unique specimen of *Shehuo* performance that straddles many cultural contents, such as history, religion, folk custom, art, etc. As for the origin of the paper platform *Shehuo* performance, there is a local explanatory tradition.

According to legend, around 2,000 BC in Chinese history, when Yu the Great came to tame

Pic. 32　Paper Platforms Illustrated by Mathew Russell

现在的礼泉县西王禹村，发现这里洪水成灾，淹没庄稼房舍，百姓性命难保。大禹为拯救苦难的百姓，率领治水大军废寝忘食，连续奋战七天七夜挖沟排水，但因水势凶猛，收效甚微。玉皇大帝被大禹的治水精神所感动，于是派他的七个女儿于正月二十三下凡相助。只见仙女们各踩一朵祥云从天而降，人人舒展广袖，立见一道河谷出现，大水哗哗流入河谷，水灾终于平息了。为纪念大禹和七仙女的治水之恩，村名由此改为西王禹村，村西一条大禹走过的路被人们称为"禹路"，村南的排水河谷被人们称为"霄河"。后来，人们还在村中建青云寺一座，内有禹王殿、王母庙等。每年正月二十三为青云寺古会，村中男女老幼

the flood in the place now known as Xiwangyu Village in Liquan County, he found that the deluge had submerged crops and houses and the locals were struggling to survive. In order to rescue the people from their sufferings, Yu the Great led his hydraulic team for seven days and seven nights in a battle to dig enough drainage ditches. Owing to the ferocity of the flood waters, their efforts had little effect. The Jade Emperor was moved by his determination to tame the flood, so he sent his seven daughters to help him on the 23rd day of the first lunar month. Riding on auspicious clouds, the fairies descended from the heavens and stretched out their gaping sleeves. Suddenly, a river valley opened up, and the floods emptied into the river. Finally, the peril subsided. To commemorate the generosity of Yu the Great and the seven fairies, the village changed its name to Xiwangyu Village. The road that Yu the Great walked in the west of the village was called "Road of Yu the Great", and the drainage channel in the south of the village was renamed the "River Xiao". Later on, people built a Qingyun Temple in the village, which contains the Yuwang Hall and the Wangmu Temple and so on. The 23rd day of the first lunar month marks the ancient fair of the Qingyun Temple. On that day men and women, the old and young alike, will go to the

都要去寺中祭拜。

　　纸台表演时，村中的姑娘们身穿七仙女的戏服，上妆戴花，扮成仙女模样，场地中间有四个掌灯之人，四人围成正方形，"仙女"们随着鼓点不断变换队形围绕四盏灯进行表演，取意仙女下凡，保佑村子平安。再用白纸糊成一米见方的纸框，中间留有一尺见方的小框，"仙女"们两腿站于其内，随着鼓点碎步而行，飘飘忽忽，如踩白云，几十个人不断变换队形，甚为壮观。新中国成立后虽然寺院被毁，祭祀活动也不再进行，但正月二十三的古会和走纸台这一习俗却依然保留了下来，走纸台也由晚上改为白天，四盏灯也变为四面旗。西王禹村纸台已列入陕西省第三批非物质文化遗产名录。

temple to venerate Yu.

In the paper platform performance, the girls from the village dress up as the seven fairies with flowers on their heads. Four of them form a square, holding lanterns in the middle of the performing area. The other "fairies" dance around the four lanterns and change their formations according to the pattern of the drumbeats. This signifies their descent to the earth and their blessing the village. The village artists model white cardboard into square frames with each side one metre in length, leaving the middle part a smaller frame for "fairies" to stand within on their legs and walk with the drumbeats like stepping on white clouds. Dozens of "fairies" constantly change performing formations, which appears quite spectacular. Although the temple was destroyed after 1949 and the sacrificial rites fell into abeyance, the customs of the ancient fair and the paper platform performance on the 23rd day of the first lunar month were well preserved. The paper stage performance was rescheduled from night to day, and the four lanterns were exchanged for four flags. The Paper Platform of Xiwangyu Village was listed among the third batch of the Intangible Cultural Heritage in Shaanxi Province.

3.4 渭城区二月二古庙会

The Ancient Temple Fair on the Lunar February 2nd in Weicheng District

咸阳市渭城区渭阳街道办事处双泉村的二月二古庙会是一个具有丰富民俗文化内涵的文化空间形式。双泉村早先的药王洞在现今的双泉小学里。主要建筑为倚原而挖出的土窑洞。在土窑洞里供奉着药王孙思邈的塑像。据传唐朝时，有一年大病流行，药王孙思邈在这里治病救人。为了加快治疗速度，让人们在需要时随时随地能吃上药，药王就把自己研制的中药夹在面里，做成豆子形状，经过翻炒，制成馍豆散发给大家食用。大家吃了药王发的炒馍豆，病很快就好了。这里的百姓为了纪念药王孙思邈，就修了这座寺庙。原药王洞在20世

The ancient temple fair on the lunar February 2nd in Shuangquan Village, Weiyang Sub-district Office, Weicheng District, Xianyang City, is an institution that embraces rich folk cultural connotations. In ancient times, the Yaowang (King of Medicine) Cave in Shuangquan Village was situated on the site now occupied by Shuangquan Primary School. The main chambers were to be found in the earthen caves excavated from the plateau cliff. A statue of Sun Simiao, the King of Medicine, was enshrined inside. It is said that an epidemic broke out during the Tang Dynasty (618–907) and the King of Medicine, Sun Simiao, came here to cure the illness and save local residents. In order to accelerate the treatment and allow people to take the medicine anytime and anywhere when they needed it, Sun Simiao worked the drugs into a flour and fashioned them into bean-shaped bread buns. After stir-frying them, they were distributed to people to eat. Once consumed, the treatment proved remarkably efficacious. Therefore this temple was built to commemorate Sun Simiao, the King of Medicine. The original Yaowang

纪 50 年代已毁，大殿也被拆除。20 世纪 80 年代，当地群众利用一个防空洞供奉药王，后集资修建了五间大房，供奉着药王孙思邈、送子娘娘、玉皇大帝等。

渭城区二月二古庙会一般历时三天。由附近的八寨五村共同主办，每年有一个主会领衔操办。二月初一这天，各村寨就前来供奉。庙前设香案，每来到一个村寨，锣鼓相送相迎，场面宏大，蔚为壮观。二月二正会这天，各村寨必进香朝拜，最引人注目的是各村寨的锣鼓、社火、秧歌表演。主办村寨还要唱三天三夜大戏。在朝拜活动中，人们还要诵经，《劝世歌》是人们最喜欢诵唱的，其主要内容是"劝世人做好事多行方便，积阴功为儿孙辈辈平安"，并批评恶人恶行

Cave was destroyed in the 1950s, and the grand hall was also dismantled. In the 1980s, the local people worshipped the King of Medicine in an air-raid shelter. Later on, funds were raised to construct five large rooms to enshrine the King of Medicine, the Goddess Baby-Bestower and the Jade Emperor, et al.

The ancient temple fair on the lunar February 2nd in Weicheng District generally lasts for three days. It is co-sponsored and organised by the eight stockaded villages and five hamlets nearby, with one as the host village every year. On the first day of lunar February, all villages will come to worship. An incense table is placed in front of the temple. Gongs and drums welcome and see off the residents of each village. The scene is magnificent and spectacular. The temple fair starts from the 2nd day of lunar February, each village must offer incense and worship. The most notable components are the gongs and drums, the *Shehuo* performance and *yangge* dance. In the host village opera performances will be held for three days and three nights. In the course of the worship activities, people also chant sutras, with the *Song of Exhortation* being a favourite among the people. Its main content is to "advise folks to do good deeds and accumulate *yingong* (a good deed

和只顾金钱，破坏邻里团结的行为等。上布施也是一项必不可少的活动内容，布施者的姓名被一一录于簿中，然后领取一条红布。据说红布可以辟邪祛病，保健康平安。庙会期间还要向游人发馍豆，所发馍豆多达300公斤。

庙会的第三天，由当年主会的村寨向第二年主会的村寨移交有关办会的事宜，下一届主会的村寨要请自乐班热闹一番。至此，三天的二月二古庙会方算结束。为了保护二月二庙会，咸阳市渭城区文体事业局制定了五年（2011—2015）保护计划，并成立了保护领导小组。渭城区二月二古庙会已列入陕西省第三批非物质文化遗产名录。

to the doer's credit in the next world) to bless their offspring". It also criticises evildoers who only care about money and undermine harmony among neighbours, etc. Offering alms is also a prerequisite activity. The name of the donor will be recorded in a register, and they will then receive a piece of red cloth. It is said that the fabric can ward off evil and eliminate disease, thereby ensuring people's health and safety. During the temple fair, more than 300 kilos of bread-bun beans will be distributed among visitors.

On the third day of the temple fair, the host village will hand over the paraphernalia to the next host village. A local self-entertaining opera club will be invited by the next host village for performance to inform the public its taking over of the next temple fair business. The three-day 2nd February ancient temple fair in Weicheng District thus draws to a formal close. To protect the temple fair tradition, the Cultural and Sports Bureau of Weicheng District, Xianyang City formulated a five-year (2011−2015) protection plan and a steering group was established accordingly. The Ancient Temple Fair on the Lunar February 2nd in Weicheng District was listed among the third batch of the Intangible Cultural Heritage in Shaanxi Province.

3.5 彬县灯山庙会
The Mount Lamp Temple Fair in Bin County

彬县水帘灯山地处泾河川道，石窟开凿在泾河南岸的石崖峭壁上，西侧有水帘河流过。灯山被誉为"明岨翚金"，与之相邻的水帘河被誉为"漆溪映月"。这里自古为当地的风景名胜。

相传，花果山上原先凿有许多大小不等的石窝。唐贞观年间，为了庆贺太平盛世，祈求年年风调雨顺，人们在距花果山下百十米左右的石山上，又开凿了大大小小的石窝，大者洞口约15平方厘米，小者洞口约10平方厘米，连同以往开凿的石洞，共计1 700多个。自明代隆庆年间创始灯山庙

Mount Lamp in Shuilian Village, Bin County is located on the River Jing Valley. Its grottoes were excavated out of the rocky cliffs on the south bank of the River Jing, with the River Shuilian flowing to the west. Mount Lamp is honoured as "Ming ju hui jin" (a name descriptive of the steep gradient of the mountain and the shining colours of the mountain when lamps are illuminated), and the adjacent River Shuilian is known as the "Qi xi ying yue" (a reference to how the moon is reflected in the river at night). It has been a local scenic spot since ancient times.

According to legend, many stone nests of varying sizes were carved into the mountain. During the Golden Age of Zhenguan (627−649) in the Tang Dynasty, in order to celebrate the peaceful and prosperous times and pray for the future, people excavated large and small stone nests on the rocky mountain about 100 metres below the mountain. Large grottoes measure around 15 square centimetres and small ones around 10 square centimetres. Together with earlier specimens the stone grottoes number about 1,700. The Mount Lamp Temple Fair was founded during the Longqing Period (1567−1572)

Pic. 33　Candle Caves Illustrated by Mathew Russell

会以来，每年元宵之夜，人们都要在石窝里点燃油灯，祈求风调雨顺，合家安康。是日夜晚，远远望去，花果山上尽是灯的海洋，"灯山"之名由此而来。

正月十五灯山庙会的第一个内容是点灯山。每年农历正月十三，点灯人就要上山搭好点灯架，放上瓷灯碗，压上新灯捻，添上菜籽油，当晚点亮12盏正灯和通往"九曲十八洞"的各盏路灯；十四日晚，再点燃"轿顶

of the Ming Dynasty and since then people have lit oil lamps in the caves on the night of Lantern Festival each year to pray for good weather for the crops and well-being for families. That night, the mountain appears just like a sea of lamps, hence the name "Mount Lamp".

The first procedure in the temple fair, held on the 15th day of the first lunar month, is lighting up the mountain. Every year on 13th day of the first lunar month, the lighter will set up the light stand, put on a porcelain lamp bowl, twist a fresh wick, add rapeseed oil, and light up the front twelve lamps, as well as the different street lamps leading to different caves at that night. On the evening of the 14th day of that month, the "Sedan Top lamp" and the "Triones lamp" are lit up. On

灯"和"北斗七星灯"。正月十五夜晚，点灯仪式达到高潮，花果山上灯火通明，各洞灯光交相辉映，流光溢彩，依次构成寺院、雷峰塔、北斗七星、轿顶、牌楼等图案。那飘忽不定、如梦似幻的图案，犹如云霞中的海市蜃楼一般，更添奇趣。

灯山庙会的第二个内容是燃放花炮烟火。元宵之夜，明月当空，天朗气清，傍晚时分，万千游人聚集在灯山之下。晚上9时左右，在欢快热烈的锣鼓声中开始燃放花炮烟火。顿时花炮声震天动地，缤纷的烟火在夜空闪光。

第三个内容是敬神。孙悟空是民间祭祀的主神，陪祀的有药

the night of the 15th, the lighting ceremony reaches its climax. The lamps on the mountain are extraordinarily bright, and the lights of the caves complement one another in their radiance and beauty, which in turn imitate the outlines of real-life structures such as temples, the Leifeng Pagoda①, the Big Dipper, a sedan roof and archway. Such fluttering, dreamlike and illusory patterns resemble a mirage amid a sea of clouds, making the scene even more fantastically interesting.

The second stage of the temple fair involves setting off fireworks. On the night of Lantern Festival, the bright moon hangs in the clear sky. In the evening, thousands of tourists gather under Mount Lamp. At about 9 p.m., people begin to set off fireworks to the cheerful and enthusiastic sound of gongs and drums. All of a sudden, the din of firecrackers shakes the universe, with colourful rockets flashing in the evening sky.

The third stage of the temple fair entails worshipping the immortals. The Monkey King is the major god within this folk worship,

---

① Leifeng Pagoda is a five story tall tower with eight sides, located on Sunset Hill south of the West Lake in Hangzhou, Zhejiang, China. Originally constructed in the year 975, it is the oldest colorful bronze pagoda in China.

王、财神,十里八乡的善男信女纷纷前来进香。许愿、还愿的天灯腾空而起,寄托着人们对儿女的期望、对父母的祝愿,饱含着丰收的喜悦和合家的欢乐。

近年来,由于灯山庙会活动形式缺乏创新,原始的灯山效果同现代光电技术相比大为逊色,参观人数急剧下降。加之许多庙会的组织者相继辞世,出现了后继乏人的情况。彬县灯山庙会已列入陕西省第三批非物质文化遗产名录。

accompanied by the King of Medicine and the God of Wealth. Devout men and women from nearby villages all come to offer incense. The lamps ascending into the sky signify the making and redeeming of vows. They bear people's expectations for their children, wishes for their parents, and the joy of harvest and reunion.

In recent years, owing to a lack of innovation in the form of activities, this low-tech lamp display has come to be seen as anachronistic and primitive. The number of visitors has tailed off sharply. In addition, many temple fair organisers have passed away one after another, resulting in a paucity of successors. The Mount Lamp Temple Fair in Bin County was listed among the third batch of the Intangible Cultural Heritage in Shaanxi Province.

3.6 姜嫄庙会
The Jiang Yuan Temple Fair

陕西省杨凌区揉谷镇姜嫄村是华夏圣母姜嫄的受封地,也是农业始祖后稷的诞生之地。

As well as being the feudatory of the Chinese Holy Mother Jiang Yuan, Jiangyuan Village in Rougu Town, Yangling District, Shaanxi Province is also the birthplace of the

姜嫄祠位于姜嫄村南边，紧邻村庄，坐北面南，与秦岭遥相呼应。

姜嫄祠至今已有4 000余年的历史。在漫长的岁月中，姜嫄祠曾经三毁四建。据祠中碑文记载，明代武功人康海于正德壬申年将此祠修复一新，曰姜嫄古寺。清代祠曾被烧毁，圣母殿独存。光绪年间，重修姜嫄寺。复修后的姜嫄寺殿宇宏伟，楼阁重叠，飞檐斗拱，金碧辉煌。但在"文化大革命"中，寺中建筑大多被拆除，仅留圣母殿。

现在的姜嫄祠修建于2001年10月。圣母殿祀奉圣母姜嫄塑像，壁画为姜嫄履迹生子、教民稼穑的故事。下殿七间，祀奉后稷、公刘、太王、文王、武

progenitor of agriculture Hou Ji. Located in the south of Jiangyuan Village, Jiang Yuan Temple stands next to the village, facing south and echoing the Qinling Mountains from a distance.

With over 4,000 years of history, the Jiang Yuan Temple has been destroyed three times and reconstructed four times. According to the inscription on the tablets within the temple, Kang Hai, a native of Wugong County in the Ming Dynasty, rebuilt the temple and named it the Jiang Yuan Ancient Temple in 1512. The temple was burned down in the Qing Dynasty, and only the Holy Mother Hall survived the fire. It was rebuilt in the reign of the Emperor Guangxu (1875–1908). After reconstruction, the new Jiang Yuan Temple stood out because of its splendid and magnificent pavilions with corniced brackets. But during the Cultural Revolution (1966–1976) most of the temple buildings were demolished, leaving only the Holy Mother Hall.

The current Jiang Yuan Temple was finished in October 2001. The Holy Mother Hall enshrines a statue of Jiang Yuan, while the mural depicts the story of how Jiang Yuan bore a son by stepping the Heavenly God's giant footprints and how Jiang Yuan taught people about farming. There are seven lower halls enshrining statues of

王、周公等圣人塑像。山门两层，下为门道，上层祀奉姜太公塑像。2002年（壬午年）正月二十三举行了隆重的开光仪式。

姜嫄庙每逢初一、十五、六月、腊月都有当地群众前去进行祭拜活动，尤以每年正月二十三的庙会规模最为宏大，姜嫄村及其周边八社十六村的群众纷纷前来参加。庙会期间有宣读祭文、游村赐福、求子导学、还愿吃面、许愿酬神、敬香唱戏等活

saints, such as Hou Ji[①], Gong Liu[②], Tai Wang[③], King Wen of Zhou[④], King Wu of Zhou, Duke of Zhou[⑤]. The two-layered entrance gate consists of a doorway on the lower layer and the statue of Jiang Taigong on the top layer. The grand opening ceremony was held on 23rd January 2002 according to the Lunar Calendar.

Local people come to the temple to worship on the 1st and the 15th day of each month. June and December of the Lunar Calendar witness more activities of this kind. The temple fair on the 23rd day of the first lunar month is the largest in scale with people in Jiangyuan Village and the surrounding villages as well participating in the magnificent fair. The temple fair includes activities, such as reading out an elegiac address, patrolling the community and offering blessings, praying for children, guiding students, votiving vows and

---

① Hou Ji was a legendary Chinese culture hero credited with introducing millet to humanity during the time of the Xia Dynasty (2070 BC–1600 BC).
② Gong Liu or Duke Liu was a noble of ancient China. He was an important early leader of the Ji clan, which later founded the Zhou Dynasty (1046 BC–256 BC).
③ meaning "the greatest of all kings". He was the grandfather of the King Wen of Zhou.
④ King Wen of Zhou was Count of Zhou during the late Shang Dynasty in ancient China. He was posthumously honored as the founder of the Zhou Dynasty and titled king though it was his son, King Wu of Zhou Dynasty defeated the King Zhou of Shang and overthrown the Shang Dynasty (1600 BC–1046 BC).
⑤ His personal name is Ji Dan (therefore called Zhou Gong Dan), was the brother of the founder of the Zhou Dynasty, King Wu of Zhou. Both were the sons of King Wen of Zhou.

动,内容丰富,形式多样,表达了人们对姜嫄、后稷等上古先民和造福百姓的英雄人物的敬仰之情。姜嫄庙会活动承载着渭河流域许多重大的历史文化信息,具有很高的历史价值、文化价值、学术价值和旅游价值。姜嫄庙会已列入陕西省第三批非物质文化遗产名录。

eating noodles, making a vow and recompensing deities, burning incense and performing operas. These rich and diverse activities express people's reverence for ancestors and heroes who bless the people, such as Jiang Yuan and Hou Ji. The Jiang Yuan Temple Fair is a major repository for historical and cultural information from the area around the River Wei, and has high historical, cultural, academic and touristic value. The Jiang Yuan Temple Fair was listed among the third batch of the Intangible Cultural Heritage in Shaanxi Province.

3.7 灵山庙会
The Mount Lingshan Temple Fair

凤翔灵山庙会是佛道合一的庙会。灵山既有阿弥陀佛禅院、铁佛禅院、观音禅院、孤魂禅院等四座佛教禅院,又有属于道教的老母宫。佛事活动与道教活动在灵山相融共生。

据传,灵山庙中所供奉的老母,就是人文始祖炎帝的母亲女登。

The Mount Lingshan Temple Fair in Fengxiang County integrates Buddhist and Taoist elements. Mount Lingshan is home to four Buddhist monasteries including the Amitabha Monastery, the Iron Buddha Monastery, the Bodhisattva Monastery, and the Wandering Souls Monastery, as well as the Taoist Laomu Palace. Buddhist and Taoist activities show themselves to be compatible at Mount Lingshan.

It is said that the identity of the Laomu worshipped at the Mount Lingshan Temple is Nüdeng, the mother of the Yan Emperor, the

因其晚年居住灵山，于四月初一去世，四月初一这一天也就成了她的纪念日。灵山庙会农历四月初一为正会。但在正会前数日，陕西关中西部各县市，特别是兴平、周至、乾县、礼泉、武功等地以及甘肃的华亭、安口、平凉，宁夏的固原等地，群众便陆续赶来，直到会后才散去。灵山庙会内容丰富，除宗教活动外，民俗活动丰富多彩，祈子遗风至今不绝。物资交流规模宏大，文艺演出形式多样，县境内所有小曲班社皆以能在灵山庙会唱通宵戏为荣。

凤翔灵山庙会是陕西省内最具影响力的庙会之一，属原始的人文祭祀范畴，是研究关中地区乃至西北地区历史、人文和民俗文化发

ancestor of humanity. She lived at Mount Lingshan in her later years and died on the 1st day of the fourth lunar month, so 1st April became her anniversary. The Mount Lingshan Temple Fair formally commences on the 1st day of the fourth lunar month. However, a few days before the temple fair starts, many residents of counties and cities in the central and western part of Shaanxi, especially the counties of Xingping, Zhouzhi, Qian, Liquan, and Wugong, as well as counties like Huating, Ankou, Pingliang in Gansu Province, and Guyuan in Ningxia Province, will congregate here one after another and not disperse until the fair ends. The Mount Lingshan Temple Fair is rich in content. In addition to religious activities, there are also vibrant and colourful folk activities, and the tradition of praying for children continues to this day. The exchange of materials is large and the forms of theatrical performances are diverse. Small theatre troupes in the county are proud to be able to sing all-night operas at the Mount Lingshan Temple Fair.

The Mount Lingshan Temple Fair in Fengxiang County is one of the most influential temple fairs in Shaanxi Province. It belongs to the category of primitive humanistic sacrifice, and is a "living fossil" for studying the development and evolution of history, humanities and folk

展演变的"活化石"。灵山庙会已列入陕西省第三批非物质文化遗产名录。

culture in the Guanzhong area and even the Northwest region. The Mount Lingshan Temple Fair in Fengxiang County was listed among the third batch of the Intangible Cultural Heritage in Shaanxi Province.

3.8 龙门洞庙会
The Longmen Cave Temple Fair

陇县龙门洞庙会是以丘处机创建全真教龙门派的道教祭祀活动为主体，融群众祭祀、庆典民俗、游山赏景、娱乐、饮食等活动为一体的庙会文化活动。

The Longmen Cave Temple Fair in Long County features mainly Taoist sacrificial activities of the Longmen Cave Lineage of the Quanzhen School of Taoism, established by Qiu Chuji, a Taoist priest famed for his martial prowess. The temple fair cultural activity integrates mass sacrifices and celebrations. It is also a good opportunity for people to climb the mountain, to enjoy the landscape, and to taste local food.

龙门洞庙会历史悠久。据史料记载，龙门洞庙会始于春秋时期，建于西汉，盛于金元时期。西周大夫尹喜弃职归山隐居于此。西汉建信侯娄景晚年幽居于

The Longmen Cave Temple Fair has a storied history. According to historical records, rising in the Spring and Autumn Period (770 BC–476 BC), it was formally established in the Western Han Dynasty (202 BC–8 CE) and flourished in the Jin (1115–1234) and Yuan Dynasties (1206–1368). Yin Xi, a Grand Master[①] in the Western Zhou

---

① The *Chou Rituals* suggests that aristocratic officials were subject to a sophisticated system of personnel administration. Generally, aristocrats in the service of the King or the Feudal Lords were graded in three large categories, in descending order of rank: Ministers (*qing* 卿), Grand Masters (*da fu* 大夫), and Servicemen (*shi* 士).

此。八仙中的钟离权、吕洞宾、韩湘子在此修道炼丹。道家信徒孙思邈辞诏不受，潜山居洞，采药行医，悬壶济世。全真教龙门派"七真人"中的丘处机，创立龙门派全真道教，受金、元两代帝王的尊崇，被授予全国道教"教皇"。

龙门洞庙会活动规模较大。每年农历三月初一至四月初八，共历时40余天，有宝鸡、西安、天水、平凉等地区各县、乡镇、村组的几十万男女群众赶赴庙会。由于道教龙门派是

Dynasty (1046 BC–771 BC), abandoned his post and returned to this mountain to live in seclusion. Marquis Lou Jing in the Western Han Dynasty, lived here in his later years. Three of the Eight Immortals (*Ba Xian*[①]), named Zhongli Quan, Lü Dongbin and Han Xiangzi, cultivated themselves and practiced alchemy at this site. In defiance of an imperial edict, Sun Simiao, a believer in Taoism, spent time here collecting curative and life-saving herbs. Qiu Chuji, one of the Seven Immortals, duly established the Longmen Sect of Quanzhen Taoism. He was revered by the emperors of the Jin and Yuan Dynasties, honoured as the "Pope" of Taoism throughout the country.

The Longmen Cave Temple Fair takes place on a relatively large scale. It lasts for more than forty days from 1st March to 8th April of the Lunar Calendar. Hundreds and thousands of men and women, from various counties, towns and villages in Baoji, Xi'an, Tianshui, Pingliang, and other regions, pour into the event. As the Longmen Lineage of Taoism is where Taoism originated,

---

① In Chinese mythology, the Ba Xian, or Eight Immortals, are a group of legendary heroes who fight for justice and vanquish evil. Most of them are said to have been born in the Tang or Song Dynasty. Popular as an important part of Chinese oral history, they are revered by the Taoists and are also a popular element in secular Chinese culture. The Eight Immortals are comprised of Cao Guojiu, Han Xiangzi, He Xiangu, Lan Caihe, Li Tieguai, Lü Dongbin, Zhang Guolao, and Zhongli Quan.

3 陕西省第三批非物质文化遗产名录中的民俗
The Folk Culture in the Third Batch of the Intangible Cultural Heritage in Shaanxi Province | 143

全国道教的祖庭，每年有陕西、甘肃、山东、河北、内蒙古、湖北、四川、安徽等 13 省的道院及群众前来赶会，13 省的道院道长均在 13 个台阶上受昭分禅。龙门洞全真教在国外也名声远扬，先后有法、德、英、俄、蒙古国、印度、瑞士、朝、韩、日、新加坡、菲律宾等国的几千名信徒前来寻迹问祖。如 2008 年 4 月，美国各州道院共 23 人专程来龙门洞朝会。

龙门洞庙会活动形式多样，包括庙宇竣工时的庆典、塑像建成的开光、五腊会、上九会、天官会、太上祖师会、无量祖师会、东麻会、三霄圣母会、关圣帝君会、上元地官会、水官会等庙会祭祀活动。祭祀过程中有升幡、祭幡、立法坛、清坛、迎神、各下院送

Taoist disciples and ordinary people from 13 provinces, like Shaanxi, Gansu, Shandong, Hebei, Inner Mongolia, Hubei, Sichuan, Anhui, come to participate in the fair. On the way from the gate of the Jingfu Mountain to the Major Hall of the temple, 13 stairs were built for the 13 Taoist leaders from the 13 above mentioned provinces to stand on during the sacrificial ceremony. The Longmen Cave Lineage of Quanzhen Taoism is also well-known abroad. Thousands of Taoist believers from France, Germany, Britain, Russia, Mongolia, India, Switzerland, North Korea, South Korea, Japan, Singapore and the Philippines have come here to worship. For example, in April 2008, 23 believers from temples in the US made a special trip to the Longmen Cave Temple Fair.

The Longmen Cave Temple Fair embraces various elements, including ceremonies to consecrate new temples, on the unveiling of new statues, and on the major sacrificial festivals of Taoism, such as the *Wula* Festival (respectively celebrated on the lunar Jan. 1st, May 5th, Jul. 7th, Oct. 1st, and Dec. 8th), the Shangjiu Festival (celebrated on the lunar Jan. 9th), the Heavenly God Festival (celebrated on the lunar Jan. 15th), the Immeasurable Buddha Festival, and the Three Holy Mothers Festival. The relevant rituals comprise raising and revering streamers, erecting and clearing altars,

贡、诵经等活动。

龙门洞庙会期间，也牵动着周边的下院庙会活动。如石拱寺、火烧庵、药王洞、九龙山、悬寿山、禅儿山、闫家庵等庙会，各院逢会期间均由龙门洞寺院下派道士主持各院的祭祀活动。

龙门洞道教是元代国师丘处机在龙门洞栖居时创建的全真道教派。它以老子的自然天

welcoming the gods, offering tributes, chanting sutras, etc.

The Fair has also influenced the temple fair activities in the surrounding lower Taoist courts, such as the Shigong Temple, the Huoshao Nunnery, the Yaowang Cave, Mount Jiulong, Mount Xuanshou, Mount Chan'er, and the Yanjia Nunnery. During the Longmen Cave Temple Fair, these temples also conduct sacrificial rituals, which should be hosted by the Taoist priests from the Longmen Cave Temple.

Longmen Cave Taoism, as a Taoist Sect, belongs to Quanzhen Taoism. It was founded by Qiu Chuji, the state mentor of the Yuan Dynasty (1271−1368), when he lived in the Longmen

Pic. 34　Taoist Clergies Illustrated by Mathew Russell

道观为主，强调人们在思想、行为上应效法道教的"生而不有、为而不恃、长而不宰"的思想。它主张三教合一的思想，以儒家《孝经》、老子的《道德经》、佛教的《心经》作为该教派的必读经典。

龙门洞庙会以老子的自然天道观为主，主张"三教合一"的思想，劝教人们遵守道德行为准则，约束人们的行为，和谐人们彼此关系。要人们消除杂念邪欲，以辩证客观的思想道德教育人，对社会安定和谐有促进作用，有重要的思想道德教育价值。

龙门洞庙会活动对宗教音乐、民俗活动、

Cave. His Taoism is mainly based on Laozi's view on nature and the *Tao*, emphasising that, in thought and behaviour, people should follow the Taoist principles that "(the *Tao*) produces them and makes no claim to the possession of them; it carries them through their processes and does not vaunt its ability in doing so; it brings them to maturity and exercises no control over them". It advocates the fusion of three ideologies, with the Confucian *Classic of Filial Piety* (*Xiao jing*), *Tao Te Ching* of Laozi and the *Heart Sutra* (*Xin jing*)[①] of Buddhism as its classics.

Taking Laozi's teachings as its foundation, the Longmen Temple Fair advocates a combination of Confucianism, Buddhism and Taoism, educating people to obey behavioural principles, restricting instances of disobedience and encouraging interpersonal relationships to be more harmonious. On the other hand, it cultivates people to eradicate evil ideas by means of dialectical thinking. It thereby has great value for ideological and moral education, as well as promoting the stability and harmony of society.

In addition, the temple fair activities are invaluable in exploiting, inheriting, and developing

---

① The *Heart Sutra* (*Xin jing*) is a popular sutra in Mahayana Buddhism. In Sanskrit, the title *Prajnaparamitahrdaya* translates as "The Heart of the Perfection of Wisdom".

民间艺术等方面有挖掘、传承、发展的价值；对弘扬中国宗教文化，对联系省外、国外人际交流，有重要的对外交流价值；龙门洞庙会中的天然奇观，有得天独厚的观赏、旅游价值；龙门洞庙会的规模范围较大，有吸引群众参与庙会文化生活的参与价值；龙门洞庙会历史悠久，内容丰富，有重要的人文资料价值；龙门洞庙会期间，品种繁多的饮食小吃，有传承、发掘饮食文化的价值。龙门洞庙会已列入陕西省第三批非物质文化遗产名录。

religious music, customs activities and folk art. Meanwhile, they assist in spreading China's religious culture and communicating with the people from other provinces and countries. The marvellous spectacles endowed by nature within the temple have both unique ornamental and tourist value. Moreover, there is participatory value too. Since the fair is so large in scale it entices people to take part in the cultural life of the temple. With such a long history and rich contents, the temple fair also enjoys significant humanistic value as a repository for further research. All kinds of food and snacks are also to be seen at the fair. This endows the event with the function of being a valuable medium for inheriting and exploring culinary culture. The Longmen Cave Temple Fair was listed among the third batch of the Intangible Cultural Heritage in Shaanxi Province.

3.9 二月二庙会

The Lunar February 2nd Temple Fair

大荔县八鱼乡阿寿村坐落在洛河南岸的沙苑腹地。据传，唐时阿寿村是唐王李世民的围

Ashou Village, Bayu Township, Dali County is located in the hinterland of Shayuan on the south bank of the River Luo. It is said that Ashou Village was originally a hunting ground for Li

猎场，建有阿寿宫，后演变成一个大村落。唐代名医孙思邈晚年曾在阿寿村居住行医，治愈过许多疑难病症。后人为了纪念药王，把药王居住过的洞室修复后称为药王洞。据村中老人讲，从前药王庙中碑碣很多，曾有"明朝天启元年修"字样。据此可知，在明朝天启年间之前阿寿村的二月二庙会已经非常活跃。

阿寿村二月二古庙会历时7天，其间有接圣水、送花馍、上庙祈福、分花馍等民俗活动。其中送花馍的社火队伍浩浩荡荡，气势宏大。队前有御棍、龙旗等仪仗，还有锣鼓、花苫鼓表演，队旁有骑马的主事，同时配有两名探马。社火队伍后参加

Shimin, otherwise known as the Emperor Taizong of Tang. Here he built the Ashou Palace which later evolved into a large village. Sun Simiao, the famous doctor in the Tang Dynasty, lived and practiced medicine here in his later years, and cured many difficult diseases. In order to commemorate him, subsequent generations restored the cave where the King of Medicine lived and called it the Yaowang (King of Medicine) Cave. According to senior residents of the village, there were many steles in the Yaowang Temple, inscribed with the words "established in the first year of the Ming Dynasty". Therefore, we can deduce that the lunar February 2nd Temple Fair in Ashou Village was very active prior to the Tianqi Period (1621–1627) of the Ming Dynasty.

The ancient temple fair held here on the lunar February 2nd lasts for seven days, during which there are folk activities such as receiving holy water, offering *huamo* (decorated steamed buns), praying for blessings in the temple, and distributing *huamo*. Among these, the acrobatic and pyrotechnic troop sending *huamo* proves mighty and magnificent. At the head of the team there are guards of honour, such as royal sticks, dragon flags, as well as performances of gongs, drums and *huashan* drums. Alongside the team, there is

送花馍的群众多达四五百人，所送花馍为当地群众专为二月二古庙会制作的敬献给药王的祭品。药王庙一组面花曾在省、市、县各级举办的大赛中多次夺魁，被称为"中国一绝"。花苫鼓表演也独具特色，是民间鼓舞中一朵瑰丽的奇葩。

近年来，二月二庙会又增加了宣传推广农业科技等内容，使庙会活动更加丰富多彩。二月二庙会已列入陕西省第三批非物质文化遗产名录。

a chief on horseback and two mounted scouts. After the *Shehuo* performance, four or five hundred people participate in the delivery of *huamo*, this being the sacrifice specially made by the local people for the ancient temple fair on the lunar February 2nd. The *huamo* made for Yaowang, have won many prizes in competitions held at provincial, municipal and county levels, being hailed as "the Best in China". During the fair, the *huashan* drum performance is also unique as a magnificent and wonderful example of folk dance.

In recent years, new contents have been added to the lunar February 2nd Temple Fair in an effort to publicise and encourage the application of agricultural science and technology. These have made the event even more vibrant. The lunar February 2nd Temple Fair was listed among the third batch of the Intangible Cultural Heritage in Shaanxi Province.

3.10 鱼河堡府城隍庙庙会

The Prefect City God Temple Fair in Yuhebu Village

鱼河堡是明长城上的延绥镇36堡之一。鱼河堡原名鱼河寨，位于榆林市榆阳区，明

Yuhebu Village is one of the 36 garrisons (villages) in Yansui Town on the Great Wall built in the Ming Dynasty. Yuhebu was originally known as Yuhezhai and is located in Yuyang

成化十一年（1475），改称鱼河堡。鱼河堡府城隍庙始建于明成化九年（1473）。据传，康熙十二年（1673），康熙私访榆林卫，因鱼河城隍救驾有功，遂封为"府城隍""灵应侯"，并亲赐"灵应侯"牌匾和半朝銮驾、龙虎月牙旗以及红头伞盖一顶，命令地方官员整修庙殿。自此鱼河堡府城隍庙香火旺盛，庙宇规模逐渐扩展。"文化大革命"期间，古庙惨遭破坏，"灵应侯"牌匾下落不明。改革开放后，党的宗教政策得到贯彻落实，1983年8月，当地群众成立了新的庙会组织，开始重新修建庙宇，现已建成正殿5间，后寝宫3间，会窑30孔，神像68尊，新铸大铜香炉3个，新雕大石狮4个，

District, Yulin City. It was renamed Yuhebu Village in the 11th year of the reign (1475) of the Emperor Xianzong, while the City God Temple began to be built in the 9th year of the Emperor Xianzong's reign in 1473. Legend has it that in the 12th year of the Emperor Kangxi's reign in 1673, the Emperor paid a private visit to Yulin and was saved by the City God of Yuhe. The Emperor therefore granted the City God such titles as "Prefect City God" and "Marquis Lingying" (Lingying means "efficacious"). What is more, the Emperor personally gave him a plaque carved with the inscription "Marquis Lingying". Meanwhile, he was endowed with the privilege to use the highest level of honour guards with a flag printed with a dragon, tiger and moon, as well as a red-headed canopy. In addition, the Emperor ordered the local officials to repair the temple. From then on the Prefect City God Temple of Yuhebu received an endless stream of pilgrims, and the scale of the temple was gradually expanded. Unfortunately, the ancient temple was destroyed during the Cultural Revolution (1966–1976) with the Marquis Lingying plaque afterwards being nowhere to be found. Following the Reform and Opening Up, China's religious policy has been implemented practically. In August 1983, the local residents

石碑 6 通，并新建广场内舞台一座。

鱼河堡府城隍庙庙会活动一年举办两次，分为春香和秋香。其中以春香最为隆重，从正月初一开始至正月十六结束。正月初一，本村及其周边村庄的善男信女争先恐后地来到庙里抽签烧香上布施，以求一年的好运。正月初八是顺心日子，信徒来庙扶运，从早到晚人山人海，川流不息。正月十三城隍爷出府，出府时鼓乐齐鸣，炮声震耳，人潮涌动。队伍前的仪仗有康熙赐的半朝銮驾和龙虎月牙旗。城隍爷乘坐的八抬大红轿在开道锣声中，急奔狂跑巡

established a new temple fair organisation with the aim of restoring the holy building. Currently, there are five major halls, three rear chambers, thirty meeting grottoes, sixty-eight statues of immortals, together with three newly-forged large bronze censers, four newly-carved large stone lions, six stone tablets, as well as a stage in the new square.

The Prefect City God Temple Fair at Yuhebu Village is held twice annually, that is to say, there is a Spring Fair and an Autumn Fair. The Spring Fair is the grandest and lasts from the 1st to the 16th of January according to the Lunar Calendar. On the the 1st day of the lunar January, the devout young men and women of Yuhebu Village and surrounding communities rush into the temple to draw lots and burn incense and offer alms, praying for fortune during the entirety of the new year. The 8th day of the lunar January is considered a propitious day. Believers come to the temple to pray for personal blessings, and worshippers hustle and bustle from morning to night. On the 13th day of the lunar January the statue of the City God is carried out of the temple to the hooting of horns and the surging of crowds. The honour guards in front of the team are accompanied by the flag printed with a dragon, tiger and moon given by the Emperor Kangxi.

视检查。正月十五设灯山、灯谜、礼花、转九曲，并有社火助兴表演。正月十六吃神饭，意为保一年四季平安健康、消灾免难。

秋香从八月初一至初四，期间和尚诵《黄礼经》四天，普度众生，超度孤魂。八月初二是城隍爷的圣诞之日，出府形式与春香时相同。在鱼河堡府城隍庙庙会中，还要举办戏剧、歌舞、社火等丰富多彩的文化娱乐活动和日用工业品、农副产品交易活动。鱼河堡府城隍庙庙会已列入第三批陕西省非物质文化遗产名录。

Sitting in a big red sedan chair carried by 8 bearers, the City God begins his tour of inspection to the sound of gongs paving the way. On the 15th day of the lunar January a lantern mountain is set up. Festive activities are organised, including lantern riddles, fireworks, a *Zhuanjiuqu* lantern show and a *Shehuo* performance. Having a divine meal on the 16th day of the lunar January should ensure that the whole year to come remains safe and calamities are warded off.

As for the Autumn Fair, it lasts from the 1st to the 4th day of the lunar August with monks chanting *Huangli* sutras for four days in an effort to release all living creatures from torment. The 2nd day of the lunar August is the City God's birthday and he is paraded in a ritual similar to that of the Spring Fair. The Prefect City God Temple Fair at Yuhebu Village also involves a variety of cultural and entertainment activities, such as opera performances, songs and dances, *Shehuo* performances, as well as exchanging everyday goods and related agricultural products. The Prefect City God Temple Fair at Yuhebu Village was listed among the third batch of the Intangible Cultural Heritage in Shaanxi Province.

3.11 无量山莲云寺庙会
The Lianyun Temple Fair on Mount Wuliang

无量山莲云寺位于延安市黄龙县城西 2.5 公里处。据寺中碑文记载：莲云寺始建于明朝嘉靖三年（1524），前殿供奉释迦牟尼石雕像，后殿供奉祖师爷塑像，并将仙鹤山改为无量山，意为释迦牟尼和祖师爷功德无量。清代乾隆、嘉庆、咸丰年间三次重修，增建了"三圣洞"，每年农历七月初三举办庙会，四面八方的善男信女和各路香客上山朝拜，香火极为旺盛。民国二十八年（1939），辛亥革命元勋朱庆澜先生出资 2 000 块大洋，翻修了殿堂，重塑了佛像。

The Lianyun Temple on Mount Wuliang is located 2.5 kilometres to the west of Huanglong County, Yan'an City. According to the tablet inscriptions found inside the temple, the Lianyun Temple was founded in the 3rd year of the reign of the Emperor Jiajing of Ming in 1524. The stone statue of Sakyamuni was worshipped in the front hall, while the statue of the initiator of Buddhism was worshipped in the rear hall. The name of the mountain was changed from Xianhe (red-crowned crane) to Wuliang, signifying the boundless beneficences of Sakyamuni and the initiator. It was rebuilt three times in the Qing Dynasty, during the reigns of the Emperors Qianlong, Jiaqing and Xianfeng respectively, and a "Three-Sage Cave" was newly built. Every year on the 3rd day of the lunar July, the temple fair was held to welcome devout men and women and pilgrims from all directions scaling the mountain to worship. The aroma of incense here was all-pervasive. In the 28th year of the Republic of China era (1939), Mr. Zhu Qinglan, one of the pioneers of the Revolution in 1911, donated 2,000 silver dollars to renovate the temple and the Buddha statue.

2000年,年逾花甲的女尼释圆慧从四川来到无量山,历时10年,重修了大雄宝殿、无量祖师殿、圆通宝殿、天王殿、山门等,传统庙会的时间改到农历六月十九。

在每年庙会期间以及释迦牟尼、观世音菩萨、地藏王菩萨生日、成道日,七月十五盂兰盆会及每逢初一、十五、春节时,方圆数百里数以万计的居士、香客、信众都如期上山朝拜,祈福禳灾,祈求平安吉祥。

无量山莲云寺庙会除了祭祀活动外,已成为传统民间文化活动的展示平台。庙会期间要唱三天大戏,还要组织社火、秧歌表演等具有鲜明地域特色的舞蹈节

In 2000, Shi Yuanhui, a nun who was in her sixties transferred to Mount Wuliang from Sichuan Province, spending more than a decade reconstructing the Grand Hall, the Wuliang Patriarch Hall, the Yuantong Hall, the Heavenly King Hall, the Mountain Gate and other edifices. The date of the traditional temple fair was altered to the 19th day of June in the Lunar Calendar.

Hundreds and thousands of inhabitants, pilgrims and believers from across an area of several hundred miles will all arrive as scheduled to worship, praying that calamity be averted and blessings and safety be bestowed instead on the following occasions: (1) during the annual temple fair; (2) on the birthdays of Sakyamuni, the Guanyin Bodhisattva, and the Goddess of Earth Bodhisattva, and on the same date when they became a Buddha; (3) on the Obon Festival on the lunar 15th July; (4) on the 1st and the 15th day of each lunar month; (5) and during Spring Festival.

In addition to sacrificial activities, the Lianyun Temple at Mount Wuliang has become a platform for displaying traditional folk and cultural activities. During the temple fair, save for three days of opera performance, people also organise *Shehuo* performances, *yangge* performances, and other dances with distinct local

目，受到广大群众的热烈欢迎。此外，山货、药材、农副产品交易十分活跃，促进了地域经济的发展。

无量山莲云寺自然风光秀美、宗教文化积淀深厚，又处在华山、韩城、壶口"三点一线"旅游线上，是一处得天独厚的旅游胜地，无量山莲云寺庙活动将进一步推动黄龙旅游产业的发展。无量山莲云寺庙会已列入陕西省第三批非物质文化遗产名录。

features, which are warmly received by spectators. Furthermore, a healthy trade is done in mountain products, medicinal materials, and agricultural and sideline products, thus helping to promote the development of the regional economy.

The Lianyun Temple on Mount Wuliang boasts beautiful natural scenery and is rich in religious culture. Besides, the temple is located in a tourist axis that can be plotted between Mount Hua, Hancheng City and the Hukou Waterfall—the "three points and one line". This makes it a unique tourist destination. The activities organised during the Lianyun Temple Fair help to further promote the development of the tourist industry in Huanglong. The Lianyun Temple Fair on Mount Wuliang was listed among the third batch of the Intangible Cultural Heritage in Shaanxi Province.

3.12 延安太和山庙会
The Mount Taihe Temple Fair at Yan'an

太和山，亦称清凉山，古称莲花峰，位于延安城东，隔延河与凤凰山、宝塔山鼎足而立。太和山是中国道观圣地之一。据史料记

Mount Taihe, also known as Mount Qingliang, used to be called Lianhua (Lotus Flower) Peak. It is located in the eastern part of Yan'an and stands across the River Yan from Mount Phoenix and Mount Pagoda. Mount Taihe is one of the holy sites of Chinese Taoism. According to

载，早在隋炀帝大业三年（607），在太和山顶就修筑了莲花城。金、明、清各代都兴建或重修了众多殿宇，使太和山的规模不断扩大。数百年间，庙宇虽屡遭损毁，但"文化大革命"后经过重修，山上现有真武祖师殿、财神庙、娘娘庙、药王庙等大小殿堂65座。

太和山道观每年于正月初一至十五、四月初八、六月十三、九月初九举办四次庙会，其中四月初八的庙会最为隆重。庙会期间，除道士进行祭祀、诵经、祈祷等法事活动外，内蒙古、河南、山西、陕西、甘肃、宁夏等各地群众纷纷来此朝山进香，求神问卜，祈求平安，进行旅游和商贸文化活动，人数最多时一天达10万余人。

historical records, as early as the 3rd year of the reign of the Emperor Yang of Sui (607), Lianhua Town was constructed atop Mount Taihe. Thereafter, more temples and halls were built or rebuilt during the Jin, Ming and Qing Dynasties, serving to constantly enlarge the scale of the Mount Taihe settlement. These temples suffered the ravages of many centuries and were reconstructed after the Cultural Revolution. There are 65 temples and halls, such as the Zhenwu Patriarch Hall, the God of Wealth Temple, the Niangniang Temple and the Yaowang (King of Medicine) Temple.

The Mount Taihe Taoist Temple Fair is held four times a year, namely, (1) from the 1st to the 15th day of the lunar January; (2) the 8th day of the lunar April; (3) the 13th day of the lunar June; (4) and the 9th day of the lunar September. Among these, that organised on the 4th day of the lunar April is the grandest. During the temple fair, apart from Taoist priests performing religious rites, such as sacrificing, chanting sutras and praying, people from Inner Mongolia, Henan, Shanxi, Shaanxi, Gansu and Ningxia provinces come here to pay religious homage, offer incense, have their fortunes told and pray for safety, as well as tour and undertake business and cultural activities. At its peak, the number of attendees exceeds one hundred thousand in a single day.

每年的太和山庙会都是由当地群众自发组织，太和山庙会是集宗教、文化活动、商贸习俗为一体的民间活动，太和山庙会的活动以民间习俗和文化活动为主、具有当地传统的民俗特色。延安太和山庙会已列入陕西省第三批非物质文化遗产名录。

The annual temple fair on Mount Taihe is arranged spontaneously by local people. It is a folk event that combines religious, cultural activities and business customs. The temple fair composes mainly folk customs and cultural activities with distinct and strong local characteristics. The Mount Taihe Temple Fair at Yan'an was listed among the third batch of the Intangible Cultural Heritage in Shaanxi Province.

3.13 宁陕城隍庙会
The Ningshan City God Temple Fair

宁陕城隍庙地处宁陕县城北5公里，坐落在老城村北门外长安河沙洲之上。城隍庙院内绿树成荫，古松、古柏、竹林郁郁葱葱，与殿堂楼阁相映成趣。院外清澈的长安河水环绕庙宇四周。

宁陕城隍庙会始于

The Ningshan City God Temple is located on the alluvial plain of the River Chang'an outside the North Gate of Laocheng Village, approximately 5 kilometres to the north of Ningshan county town. The courtyard of the City God Temple is lined with luxuriantly green foliage, like pines, cypresses and bamboo groves, which form a fine contrast with its halls and pavilions. The clear waters of the River Chang'an encircle the temple beyond the courtyard.

The Ningshan City God Temple Fair began

清乾隆年间，一直延续到民国末年。中华人民共和国成立后，庙会活动曾一度中止。1994年，传统的四月八庙会活动得以恢复。宁陕城隍庙会以民间信仰活动和传统文化活动为主要表现形式，是陕南地区城隍信仰的核心活动场所。庙会前一天要举行隆重的城隍出巡仪式。从四月初七开始，在城隍庙殿前设香案做道场。道场分为祈福道场和度亡道场两大类。祈福道场为生者祈福，祈求国泰民安、风调雨顺；度亡道场为死者超度，祈求死者安息。佛、道及民间吉祥神共处一庙，香客各取所需。每年参加庙会的群众达三四万人之多，除本县群众外，石泉、汉阴、佛坪、柞水、镇安乃至西安、安康、汉中等地的群众也来赶会。每逢会

in the reign of the Emperor Qianlong in the Qing Dynasty and lasted until the closing days of the Republic of China period (1912–1949). After the founding of the People's Republic of China, temple fair activities were suspended and it was not until 1994 that the traditional temple fair on the 8th day of the lunar April was resumed. The Ningshan City God Temple Fair takes folk worship activities and traditional cultural activities as its mainstay, and this is the principal site for worshipping the City God in southern Shaanxi. On the day prior to the temple fair, there is a grand tour for the City God's patrol. From the 7th day of the lunar April, an incense table for Taoist rites is set up in front of the City God Temple Hall. The Taoist rites are divided into a prayer ritual and a ritual of deliverance. The former is targeted at the living, praying that the country will be prosperous and the people at peace, as well as for timely wind and rain; the latter is meant for the dead, petitioning that the souls of the deceased can be released from purgatory and rest in peace. The Buddha, Taoist deities and auspicious folk gods share one temple, and the pilgrims worship what they believe. As many as 30,000 or 40,000 people participate in the temple fairs each year. In addition to local residents, people also head to the

期，各路商贾云集，大小摊点密布，农副产品、百货食品交易十分活跃。庙会上的戏剧演出，农业科技普及等文化、科技活动受到群众的热烈欢迎，成为庙会的新的亮点。除传统的庙会活动外，宁陕城隍庙会也是进行物资交流和开展群众性文化活动的一个重要平台。

宁陕城隍庙会由会首组织举办，会首由庙里主持、总约、绅首等轮流担任。1994年庙会活动恢复后，由历任城隍庙文管所所长任会首，主持庙会有关事宜。宁陕城隍庙会已列入陕西省第三批非物质文化遗产名录。

temple fair from Shiquan, Hanyin, Foping, Zhashui, Zhen'an and even Xi'an, Ankang and Hanzhong. During the event, merchants from other places gather here, setting up large or small stalls, actively trading in agricultural and sideline products and other merchandise. Theatrical performances rub shoulders with cultural and technological activities, some of which aim to popularise agricultural science and technology. These have been warmly welcomed by the masses and become new highlights of the temple fair. In addition to the traditional festivities, the Ningshan City God Temple Fair also serves as an important platform for material exchanges and mass cultural activities.

The Ningshan City God Temple Fair is overseen and organised by the head of the fair, a post which is alternately occupied by the temple host, the general covenant, the county head, certain gentlemen, et al. After the resumption of the temple fair activities in 1994, this position was held by whoever served as director of the City God Temple Cultural Management Office. He or she presides over the fair and related matters. The Ningshan City God Temple Fair was listed among the third batch of the Intangible Cultural Heritage in Shaanxi Province.

3.14 彬县大佛寺三月八庙会

The Big Buddha Temple Fair on Lunar March 8th in Bin County

彬县大佛寺地处泾河川道，大佛寺石窟开凿在泾河南岸的石崖峭壁上，寺前泾河蜿蜒东流。这里风光旖旎，山清水秀。

唐初，李世民为了纪念平定薛举而战亡的将士，从武德元年(618)开始，修建豳州应福寺石窟，至贞观二年(628)基本建成。此后历代多

The Big Buddha Temple is located in the River Jing Valley. The grotto which houses the Big Buddha Temple is excavated from the cliff-face on the southern bank of the River Jing. The river in fact winds eastward in front of the holy place. All these features make the scenery here exquisite and picturesque.

In the early Tang Dynasty, the Emperor Taizong ordered the building of the Yingfu Temple Grottoes in Binzhou to commemorate the officers and soldiers who lost their lives in the battle against Xue Ju. Construction began in the first reigning year of Emperor Gaozu of Tang in

Pic. 35 The Big Buddha Temple Illustrated by Mathew Russell

有重修。据寺内题刻记载，唐称应福寺，北宋改名庆寿寺，俗称大佛寺。寺中石刻造像众多，其中尤以阿弥陀佛造像最为高大精美，故而得名。彬县大佛寺三月八庙会自古有之，民国以前为寺院主持，新中国成立后由群众自发组织，现由大佛寺石窟博物馆主持举办。彬县大佛寺庙会主要影响范围在以彬县为圆心的方圆150公里内，包括西安、咸阳、平凉等地。

彬县大佛寺三月八庙会是集宗教、文化、文物、艺术、旅游等于

618), and was basically completed in the 2nd year of Zhenguan Era[①] in 628. Since then, it has been rebuilt in many dynasties. According to the inscriptions in the temple, it was called the Yingfu Temple in the Tang Dynasty and was renamed the Qingshou Temple in the Northern Song Dynasty, though was popularly known as the Big Buddha Temple. Among the stone sculptures in the temple, the Amitabha Buddha is especially tall and exquisite, hence the name. A Big Buddha Temple Fair has been held on the lunar March 8th in Bin County ever since ancient times. Prior to the Republic of China period the event was organised by the temple itself, though after the founding of the New China its administration was transferred to local people and now falls under the aegis of the Big Buddha Temple Grotto Museum. The catchment area for the fair extends around 150 kilometres, taking in Xi'an, Xianyang, and Pingliang and other places.

The lunar March 8th Big Buddha Temple Fair in Bin County is an ancient and traditional event that blends religion, culture, cultural relics,

---

① Zhenguan is Emperor Taizong's reign title from 626 to 649, known as the Reign of Zhenguan in Chinese history. His reign is considered the first golden age of Tang Dynasty, which lays a solid foundation for the Kaiyuan Era.

一体的古老而传统的集会。相传，农历三月初八是大佛的生日，每年三月初六便有善男信女从四面八方赶来礼佛，或进香还愿，或求子祈福，或旅游观光，三月初八达到高潮，日接待游客达万人以上。庙会期间，客商云集，摊点密布，游人如织，十分热闹，有时也有戏剧演出助兴。从2010年开始，彬县依附大佛寺三月八庙会组织开展以"大佛文化"为主题的旅游节，宣传推介彬县旅游资源，迎来八方游客。现在，旅游节已成为古庙会的一个新的亮点。近年来，中央电视台《国宝档案》栏目和《陕西日报》等对彬县大佛寺庙会进行了报道，提高了庙会的知名度。彬县大佛寺三月八庙会已列入陕西省第三批非物质文化遗产名录。

art and tourism. Legend has it that the lunar March 8th is purportedly the birthday of the Big Buddha. Every year on lunar March 6th, devout men and women from all directions will come to pay their respects, offer incense, redeem their vows, pray for conception and good fortune, or go sightseeing. The climax comes on the lunar March 8th with more than 10,000 visitors received on each day of the event. During the fair, numerous merchants set up stalls and the place is packed with tourists. It is very lively and sometimes opera performances are put on for entertainment. Since 2010, Bin County has organised a tourist festival with the theme of "Big Buddha Culture", based on the fair on the lunar March 8th. This aims to promote and expand tourism in the county, welcoming visitors from all over the world. At present, the tourism festival has became a new highlight of the ancient temple fair. In recent years, the "National Treasure Archives" column of CCTV and the *Shaanxi Daily* newspaper have reported on the fair, thus boosting its reputation to some extent. The Big Buddha Temple Fair on the lunar March 8th in Bin County was listed among the third batch of the Intangible Cultural Heritage in Shaanxi Province.

3.15 苏蕙织锦回文与武功民间送手绢风俗

Su Hui Brocading Palindrome Poems on Silk and the Folk Custom of Sending Handkerchiefs as Gifts in Wugong County

苏蕙织锦回文与武功民间送手绢风俗在咸阳市武功县已经有1 600多年的历史。苏蕙,约生于前秦苻坚永兴元年(357),自幼聪颖过人,能吟诗绘画、织锦刺绣。有一次,苏蕙与父亲去法门寺逛庙会,遇到窦滔。窦滔能骑善射,武艺高强。二人一见钟情,结为夫妻。婚后夫妻十分恩爱。但好景不长,窦滔从军后,因罪被发配到流沙。后窦滔被任命为安南将军,镇守襄阳。赴任时,窦滔带走了敦煌歌女赵阳台,苏蕙不肯同行,窦滔竟与苏蕙断绝音信。苏蕙不胜伤感,每日写诗抒怀,年复一年,竟写诗7 900多首,

Su Hui brocading palindrome poems on silk and the folk custom of sending handkerchiefs as gifts have a history of more than 1,600 years in Wugong County, Xianyang City. Su Hui was born in 357 (the 1st year of the reign of the Emperor Fu Jian of the Former Qin Dynasty). From childhood, she displayed great intelligence and was adept at poetry, painting, brocading and embroidery. One day, Su Hui and her father visited the Famen Temple Fair and met Dou Tao, a skilled archer and equestrian, who excelled at martial arts. They fell in love at first sight and as newlyweds were the picture of a harmonious couple. But the good times did not last for long. After Dou Tao joined the army, he was exiled to Liusha for a crime. Later, he was appointed as General Annan to guard Xiangyang City. When he assumed his post, Dou Tao took Zhao Yangtai, a singer from Dunhuang, with him. Su Hui refused to go with them and Dou Tao broke up with her unexpectedly. Su Hui was so grieved that she wrote poems to express her feelings every day. Year after year, she composed more

用五彩丝线织成回文诗，共841字，上下左右回环往复，皆可诵读，这就是流传千古的《回文璇玑图》。苏蕙将回文诗寄给窦滔，窦滔感于苏蕙深情，便将宠妾送回扶风家中，与苏蕙和好如初。

武功民间送手绢风俗是由织锦回文演变而来的民间风俗，当地乃至关中许多地方都有在结婚当日送手绢的民间风俗。苏蕙织锦回文与武功民间送手绢风俗已列入陕西省第三批非物质文化遗产名录。

than 7,900 verses. And she wove them into palindrome poems on silk with colourful threads. The poems may be read from top to bottom or from left and right, and are comprehensible in each direction. This was the origin of the *Palindrome Picture* that has been passed down through ages. Su Hui sent the palindrome poems by postal courier to Dou Tao, who could not help but be deeply moved by her affection. He sent his concubine Zhao Yangtai back to Fufeng and reconciled with his legal wife, Su Hui.

The folk custom of sending handkerchiefs as gifts in Wugong evolved from the palindromes brocaded by Su Hui. Local people and even residents of the wider region within the passes maintain the folk custom of sending a handkerchief as a gift on their wedding day. Su Hui Brocading Palindrome Poems on Silk and the Folk Custom of Sending Handkerchiefs as Gifts in Wugong County were listed among the third batch of the Intangible Cultural Heritage in Shaanxi Province.

3.16 重阳追节送花糕

Giving Courtesy Steamed Buns as Gifts at Double Ninth Festival

重阳追节送花糕这一习俗主要流传于咸阳

The custom of giving courtesy steamed buns as gifts at Double Ninth Festival is mainly

市渭河南岸各村，并辐射周边地区。送花糕风俗历史悠久，据《西京杂记》记载，汉朝时就有在重阳节吃糕之风俗。

咸阳民间俗称给女儿追节为"走女家"。"走女家"有送花糕（用面蒸做的花馍）的礼俗，因此"走女家"也称"送花糕"。其中女儿新婚追送中秋节的"八月花糕"尤为讲究，一般要送两个花糕，用肩担挑或二人抬送。花糕呈塔形，制作工具有擀面杖、小剪刀、顶针、镊子、竹签、上色用的毛笔、六烘膏（颜料）等，寓意步步登高。糕塔以面饼分层垒成，三层、五层不限，周沿为花边，层间以大枣、核桃撑托，上层塑以盘龙或团花做顶，顶

observed in the villages on the southern banks of the River Wei around Xianyang City. It is not unknown in surrounding areas, however. This practice enjoys a long history. According to the *Miscellaneous Records of the Western Capital* (*Xi jing za ji*), it was at that time normal to consume steamed bread buns on the Double Ninth Festival.

Paying a visit to a married daughter's home has the alternative title of "walking to daughter's home" among the people of Xianyang. Customarily, courtesy steamed buns, namely decorated steamed buns, otherwise known as *huamo*, are taken as gifts on such a visit. Therefore, "visiting a daughter's home" is also known as "giving *huagao*". Among them, the "August *huagao*" of the Mid-Autumn Festival given to a newly married daughter is especially exquisite. Generally, two *huagao* are delivered by carrying pole on the bearer's shoulders or carried by two people. The *huagao* is in the shape of a tower, implying scaling up step-by-step. The tools involved in making them include rolling pins, small scissors, thimbles, tweezers, bamboo sticks, brushes for colouring, and six baking pastes (paints), etc. The tower-shape *huagao* consists of three or five layers of flat bread with a lace fringing. Dates and walnuts are embedded

3 陕西省第三批非物质文化遗产名录中的民俗
The Folk Culture in the Third Batch of the Intangible Cultural Heritage in Shaanxi Province

Pic. 36 *Huamo* Illustrated by Mathew Russell

部广插色彩艳丽的面花。面花以动物花鸟或戏剧人物构成，如"二龙戏珠""龙凤呈祥""嫦娥奔月""牛郎织女"等，这是花糕的精华部分。塔底周边以柿子和石榴造型环绕，数量以 40 个为宜，寓意事事如意。

重阳追节送花糕是

into the layers. The upper layer sports a dragon-shaped or flower-shaped pattern with lots of colourful dough adornments. The moulded dough is composed of animals, flowers and birds or characters from drama, such as "Two Dragons Playing with a Pearl", the "Dragon and Phoenix as Bringers of Prosperity", the "Goddess Chang'e Flies to the Moon", and the "Cowherd and the Girl Weaver". This is the essence of the *huagao*. The bottom layer of the "tower" is encircled by a number of persimmons and pomegranates. Forty of them are suggested, no more, no less, since the word "forty" (*sishi*) in Chinese sounds like "everything" (*shishi*), implying that everything will go smoothly.

Giving *huagao* during the Double Ninth

重阳节前娘家为初嫁的女儿追节送礼的一种民间习俗，制作精美、造型别致的"花糕"浓缩着重阳节传统的文化底蕴，彰显着吉祥喜庆的民俗文化精神，体现了传统农耕文化中劳动人民的朴实情感。目前，原流传于关中腹地广大农村的重阳追节送花糕习俗，现在只有少数农村将这一习俗流传下来。重阳追节送花糕已列入陕西省第三批非物质文化遗产名录。

Festival is a folk custom whereby the family presents gifts to their newly-married daughters before the Double Ninth Festival. The exquisitely made *huagao* in delicate patterns enshrines the traditional cultural heritage of the Double Ninth Festival, highlights the auspicious and festive cultural spirit and embodies the unsophisticated affection of the labouring people living in agrarian society. At present, the custom of giving huagao during the Double Ninth Festival, which used to be popular in the vast rural areas within the passes, has only been inherited and practiced in few villages. The custom of giving *huagao* as gifts at Double Ninth Festival was listed among the third batch of the Intangible Cultural Heritage in Shaanxi Province.

3.17 大荔乞巧节

The Qiqiao Festival in Dali County

农历七月初七，是我国民间传统的七夕节，也叫乞巧节、女儿节、双星节、巧节等。相传，在这天晚上，分居于天河两岸的牵牛星和织女星在鹊桥上相会，妇女于此夜，向织

The 7th July according to the Lunar Calendar is designated as the traditional Chinese folk Qixi Festival (Chinese Valentine's Day). Its alternative names are Qiqiao Festival, Girl's Day, Double Star Festival, and Qiao Festival. It is said that on the evening of that day, the mythological Cowherd and the Girl Weaver (in Western astronomy these correspond to the stars

女星乞求智巧。乞巧节历史悠久，五代和凝在《宫词》中就有"阑珊星斗缀珠光，七夕宫嫔乞巧忙"的记载。到唐代七夕节已变成了名副其实的女儿节。大荔县乞巧节在20世纪60年代以前已经遍及乡里。旧时，农村姑娘七夕晚上缚"巧姑"，在巷中置案，献瓜果、巧菜，祭拜巧姑。乞巧时讨巧的姑娘趴在巧姑前，用被单盖住，两旁有八人手拿两个瓷大碗，摩擦时发出刺耳之声，磨碗时间长了，姑娘中谁打瞌睡就被讥笑为笨人。待磨碗声让人发蒙时，让其起来表演剪花，看谁灵巧。"文化大革命"期间七巧节活动一度停止，2000年后又重新恢复了乞巧节。

Altair and Vega), who live on separate sides of the River Tianhe, are allowed to reunite at the Magpie Bridge. Women pray the Girl Weaver for ingenuity on this night. The Qiqiao Festival boasts a long history. He Ning of the Five Dynasties recorded in the *Poetry of the Imperial Palace* (*Gong ci*) that "few stars twinkle in the sky at night, imperial ladies pray for hands so light". By the Tang Dynasty, Qixi Festival had become a veritable institution for girls. By the 1960s the Qiqiao Festival had already come to be celebrated throughout the countryside of Dali County. In the old days, on the evening of Qixi Festival, the rural girls would make a lady of straw, called "Qiaogu"（Aunt Qiao) and set a table in the alley to offer fruits, vegetables and *qiaocai* (self-planted green onions or bean sprouts) to worship Qiaogu. When praying for ingenuity, the girls took turns to lie prostrate in front of the table to be covered with cloth sheets. On the two sides of these girls were eight people holding respectively two big bowls which they rubbed like a glass harmonica to see who could bear it the longest. Ones who dozed off during the rubbing would be considered stupid. When the contest was over, they were asked to stand up to cut paper flowers to see who was the most dexterous. Qiqiao Festival activities ceased

大荔县大壕营村妇女继承了传统的乞巧活动，如泡巧芽、蒸巧馍、缚巧姑、搭巧棚、磨巧碗、背巧歌等；还增加了展巧、赛巧活动等助兴内容，如剪纸、刺绣、民间纺织、蒸花馍、皮影表演、木偶表演、农村自乐班以及与之有关的诗联、书法、绘画现场表演等，给传统的乞巧节活动增添了新的赛巧内容。

大荔县乞巧节产生了广泛的影响。2006年，日本七夕研究会专程来大荔县考察乞巧节活动，《西安晚报》开辟专版专题讨论"大荔乞巧节"，引起了社会关注。大荔乞巧节已列入陕西省第三批非物质文化遗产名录。

during the Cultural Revolution, and then resumed after the year 2000.

The women of Dahaoying Village in Dali County have inherited the traditional activities of Qiqiao Festival, such as planting bean sprouts (*pao qiao ya*), steaming buns (*zheng qiao mo*), making Qiaogu with straw (*fu qiao gu*), building sheds (*da qiao peng*), grinding bowls (*mo qiao wan*), singing songs (*bei qiao ge*), etc. In addition, activities which show off and try to determine who has the lightest hand include paper-cutting, embroidery, folk weaving, making *huamo*, shadow play, puppet shows, local self-entertaining opera performances and creating poetic couplets, on-site exhibitions of calligraphy and painting, thereby infusing new content into the traditional activities of Qiqiao Festival.

The Qiqiao Festival in Dali County has had a profound impact. In 2006, the Japanese Qixi Research Society made a special trip to Dali County to observe the festival activities. And the *Xi'an Evening News* introduced a new column for the discussion of "Qiqiao Festival in Dali County", which attracted social attention. The Qiqiao Festival in Dali County was listed among the third batch of the Intangible Cultural Heritage in Shaanxi Province.

3.18 大荔血故事
The Bloody Dumb Show in Dali County

血故事是社火芯子中的一种，人称"武芯子"，多取材于凶杀格斗的传统武戏，如《铡美案》《王佐断臂》《耿娘仇》《刺辽王》和神鬼传说中的"鬼推磨""阎王换头""锯裂分身"等故事。血故事表演时运用独特的化装方法和特制的刀、枪、铡、剑等工具，使铡头、挖眼、割腹、剁脚、断手等血淋淋的场面在瞬间得以艺术再现，主要突出"血"的特点。这种表演形式虽然充满神秘感和血腥、恐怖的场面，但它用集中而夸张的方式教育人们多行善举，不做恶事，可以起到惩恶扬善、寓教于乐的作用，对促进和谐社会建设具有积极作用。这种"绝活"是血

The bloody dumb show, also known as the martial *Xinzi*, is one variety of acrobatic and pyrotechnic performance. At its heart is traditional mock acrobatic combat, characterised by slaying and grappling. Its scenarios include *The Execution of Chen Shimei* (*Zha mei an*), *Wang Zuo Cuts off His Own Arm* (*Wang Zuo duan bi*), *The Revenge of Mrs. Geng* (*Geng niang chou*), *Murdering the King of the Liao* (*Ci liao wang*), and legends concerning immortals and ghosts, such as "ghost grinding the mill", "the king of hell changing head", "cutting the body", etc. During the bloody dumb show, unique methods of disguise and special tools, such as broadswords, long spears, choppers, swords and so on, are used to artistically evoke bloody scenes in an instant. These might be the hacking off of heads, gouging out eyes, slicing open abdomens, and hacking off feet and hands. The "bloody" characteristics are plain to be seen. Although this performance is full of mystery, and grisly and horrible scenes, it teaches onlookers the benefits of doing good rather than evil in its full-on and exaggerated way. It plays a role in promoting righteousness and showing the wages of sin, in due course

亲单传，只传男，不传女。在表演时有许多行规和禁忌：要在保密隐蔽的环境里装扮；装扮前的一天需要淋浴，并且要隔离在社火装扮场内，不得同女人说话，不得行房事；装扮当天鸡鸣之前，装扮把式及其助手在特定的地方先将猪羊用酒馍食醉，然后秘密宰杀；装扮演员选定的化装部位要用酒清洗，然后装扮，装扮就绪后还要饮三五杯酒，方可上芯子出游；装扮的演员须是本命年人。据说，本命年的人见了刀、枪凶器可避凶险，平安度过本命年；出芯子前一天必须祭风神，以求活动过程平安。血故事的装扮技艺神秘、复杂，有传承价值，同时，对当今电视电影中凶杀流血场面的装扮具有一定的借鉴作用。

helping to promote the construction of a harmonious society. This unique skill is only passed on to the male heirs of the performers. There are many rules and prohibitions about how the dumb show should be executed. First of all, costumes should be put on in a secret and private place. Secondly, a shower should be taken a day before dressing in costume, and the performer should be isolated in the dressing room, being forbidden to talk to women or engage in sexual relations. Thirdly, before the cock crows on the day of dressing up, the make-up artist and his assistant should feed the pigs and sheep with steamed buns that have been soaked in liquor. The intoxicated animals are then secretly slaughtered. Fourthly, parts of the performer's body to which makeup will be applied should first be cleansed with alcohol. Once the makeup is completed, he should down three or five glasses of liquor before mounting the *Xinzi* platform. Fifthly, any performer should only perform in the year of his birth-sign according to the Chinese Zodiac (if it is the Year of the Pig he should have been born in the Year of the Pig, etc). It is believed that during one's birth year a person is offered supernatural protection against injury from swords and spears, and so should be allowed to pass through those twelve months without

3 陕西省第三批非物质文化遗产名录中的民俗
The Folk Culture in the Third Batch of the Intangible Cultural Heritage in Shaanxi Province

harm. Lastly, before the *Shehuo* performance on *Xinzi*, people must worship the God of the Wind to ensure the safety of the activity. The dressing technique of the bloody dumb show is mysterious and complicated. Its long tradition makes it singularly precious, yet its secrets are to be envied by modern-day special effects experts working in television and movie production.

近年来，由于追求经济效益，大荔血故事活动已停滞了近十年之久。现在，能装扮血故事的老艺人有的已经去世，健在的老艺人都已年近花甲，血故事面临后继无人的境地，亟待重新组织表演队伍，培养传承新人，使其表演活动得以恢复。大荔血故事已列入陕西省第三批非物质文化遗产名录。

For nearly ten years now, Dali County has seen no full-scale bloody dumb show since the staging is costly in economic terms. Besides, many performers have passed away with surviving artists now being in their sixties or older. Its survival is a matter of pressing urgency and new inheritors are needed to carry on its legacy. Recruiting and training fresh performance teams is a must. The Bloody Dumb Show in Dali County was listed among the third batch of the Intangible Cultural Heritage in Shaanxi Province.

3.19 华山红社火
The Mount Hua Bloody *Shehuo* Performance

华山脚下西王堡的华山红社火（又名血故事、血虎子）曾长期在

The Mount Hua Bloody *Shehuo* Performance (also known as the bloody dumb show and the bloody tiger) is staged at Xiwangbu Village at the

关中东府乃至豫晋接壤地区享有盛誉。

据传,华山红社火是王氏先人元末明初迁至华阴后,从当地祀神祭山活动中受到启发而开创的一种社火形式,并由家族世代承袭,屡演不衰,成为当地每年三月三华佗庙会、三月十五华山庙会、清明祭祖等活动中的一大盛事。民国时,这种传统民间艺术经西王堡王仰文、祝永坤等人的创新,在表演手法上有了突破性

foot of Mount Hua. It has long enjoyed a high reputation in eastern Guanzhong and even in the contiguous areas of Henan and Shanxi.

According to legend, the Bloody Dumb Show at Mount Hua is a form of *Shehuo* performance that draws inspiration from the local activities of worshipping gods and mountains. It came into being at the juncture between the Yuan and Ming Dynasties when the ancestors of the Wang family moved to Huayin. Generation after generation have inherited this tradition and it continues to be popular as one of the grand events of the Hua Tuo Temple Fair (lunar March 3rd), the Mount Hua Temple Fair (lunar March 15th) and Qingming Festival. During the Republic of China period (1912–1949), local residents of Xiwangbu, including Wang Yangwen and Zhu Yongkun,

Pic. 37 Bloody Dumb Show Illustrated by Mathew Russel

提高，成为极富视觉刺激效果的表演形式。1945年，为庆祝抗日战争胜利，西王堡华山红社火应邀进县城表演，其高超的技艺引起轰动。1947年元宵节，华山红社火在本村演出时，遭到当地国民党驻军的暴力滋扰，村民奋起反抗，夺取了这次斗争的胜利和演出的成功，西王堡华山红社火由此名声大震。新中国成立后，1956年演了一次，此后，这一社火形式便归于沉寂。改革开放后，1986年西王堡村民重操旧艺，在本村做过一次恢复性的尝试表演。直至1993年华山举办登山节，华山红社火受邀演出，赢得了数万观众的热烈欢迎。2009年，在华山举行了"纪念汶川抗震一周年"展演活动，表演了新编的独具特色的华山红社火抗震节目，中央和省、

revived the tradition. After a breakthrough in improving performance techniques, it became a visually very stimulating spectacle. In 1945, in order to celebrate victory in the Anti-Japanese War, the performance team was invited to perform in the county town. Its superb skills caused a sensation. At the Lantern Festival in 1947, during the performance of the show at Xiwangbu Village, the players were violently harassed by the local Kuomintang garrison. Villagers fought back, proving victorious and the performance was lauded. Since then, the performance has become famous. After the founding of People's Republic of China, it was performed only once in 1956, and then fell into abeyance. In 1986, after the Reform and Opening Up, residents of Xiwangbu tried to revise it, but it was not until 1993 when the team was invited to perform at a mountaineering festival that they won acclaim from tens of thousands of spectators. In 2009, an event in "Commemoration of the First Anniversary of Wenchuan Earthquake" was held at Mount Hua. A new programme concerned with earthquake relief was performed in the way of the Mount Hua Bloody *Shehuo* performance. This was reported by many central, provincial and municipal media outlets.

市多家媒体进行了报道。

西王堡位于华山脚下，华佗衣冠冢之侧，自古以来华山红社火是祀神祭山活动的重要组成部分，表演的节目有《劈山救母》《刮骨疗毒》等。华山红社火场面惊险、扮演逼真，视觉效果强烈，在演技上除静态的造型定妆外，更有动态的表演场面。在扮演造型和空间设计上，华山红社火吸收了民间芯子和传统建筑工艺的处理手法，再附之以即景生情、妙语连珠的门联、故事联等文学内容，使其雅俗共赏、文野相生，从而产生一种惨烈中见奇趣，粗犷中寓雅正，原始中出新意的审美效果。目前，西王村党支部、村委会为了传承先人技艺，保护文化遗产，专门成立了挖掘、保护、宣传组织，积极开展相关活

Xiwangbu is located at the foot of Mount Hua alongside the cenotaph of Hua Tuo. Since ancient times, the bloody show has formed an important part of the activities for worshipping gods and mountains. The performances include *Splitting the Mountain to Save Mother* (*Pi shan jiu mu*) and *Scraping the Bones to Expel Toxins* (*Gua gu liao du*) and so on. The Mount Hua Bloody *Shehuo* Performance is thrilling, vivid and shocking in its visual effects. Apart from the static modelling set-up, there are also dynamic performance scenes. In terms of modelling and spatial design, the bloody show has absorbed skills from the folk *Xinzi* performance and traditional techniques of construction. It may also incorporate drama plots drawn from literature and wonderful couplets featuring witty words or stories. These make it both elegant and popular, well-suited to both refined and popular tastes. This produces an interesting aesthetic effect. Viewers can see an unusual charm within the tragedy, an elegance within the roughness, and the novelty in the originality. At present, in order to inherit the skill of ancestors and protect local customs, the Party branch and the committee in Xiwangbu Village have established special organisations to research, protect and promote

动，扩大红社火的社会影响。华山红社火已列入陕西省第三批非物质文化遗产名录。

examples of cultural heritage. These have actively organised relevant activities to expand the social influence of the bloody *Shehuo* performance. The Mount Hua *Shehuo* Performance was listed among the third batch of the Intangible Cultural Heritage in Shaanxi Province.

3.20 定边赛驴会
The Dingbian Donkey Race Fair

陕北的农户几乎家家户户都饲养毛驴，毛驴与当地群众的生产生活息息相关，正所谓"农家有一宝是毛驴，做工碾磨驾车犁，驮载运输无穷尽，老弱妇孺皆乘骑"。赛驴会就是当地民众展示驾驭毛驴技巧的一项竞赛活动。定边赛驴会发源于三边地区，以安边为活动中心，是农耕文化与游牧文化融合、军事文化与民俗文化融合的产物。据传，赛驴会迄今已有二三百年的历史。

Raising donkeys is common among the residents of northern Shaanxi. The beast is closely tied to the lifestyle and production activities of local people. An old saying in the locality goes that "As a treasure in farmers' house, it moves devices to grind and plough. Capable of carrying loads on its back, making it well-known far and wide". The donkey race is a competition in which local people can show off their skill at handling a pack animal. The Dingbian Donkey Race Fair originated in a trilateral area (the zones being Dingbian, Anbian and Jingbian), with Anbian as its centre of activity. It manifests the fusion of agricultural life and nomadic culture, and also brings together military culture and folk culture. Rumour has it that the fair of which the donkey race forms a part has a history of two to three hundred years.

定边赛驴会一般在秋季举办庙会、牲畜交易会、物资交流会等各种集会活动时进行。赛驴会最早是以比赛驴子走和跑的速度为主，到后来发展为多种驾驭技巧的比赛，分为走驴、跑驴、夫妻赶驴、毛驴驮重和趣味骑驴等多个项目。通过此项活动能够促进社会和谐，增长智力，增进健康。定边赛驴会已列入陕西省第三批非物质文化遗产名录。

The donkey race falls in autumn and takes place together with other fair activities including the temple fair, a livestock trading fair, and an goods-exchanging fair, etc. The donkey race was originally shaped around competitions which took into account the trotting and galloping speeds of donkeys, but later multiple driving skills were involved, like walking donkeys, running donkeys, couples driving donkeys in tandem, loading donkeys and riding donkeys for fun. This activity is very helpful in making a more harmonious society, stimulating wisdom development and enhancing people's physical health. The Dingbian Donkey Race Fair was listed among the third batch of the Intangible Cultural Heritage in Shaanxi Province.

Pic. 38　Mule Cart Illustrated by Mathew Russell

3.21 绥德定仙墕娘娘庙花会
The Niangniang Temple Flower Fair in Dingxianyan Village, Suide County

娘娘庙坐落在定仙岭上定仙墕村东头，是绥德县境内最古老的庙宇之一。据碑文记载，明代成化年间，由仙岭镇腰岩峁村迁建于此，每年三月十八为庙会日。定仙墕娘娘庙花会以给娘娘敬献花树为主要会事活动。花会会期为三天，即农历三月十七、十八、十九，十八日当天为正会。花树由六个社轮流制作，每年两个社，三年轮一次。十八、十九日的花会由制作花树的两个社分别承办，十七日的花会和花树由定仙墕村何姓人家承办和年年敬献。

花会的主要仪程是三月十六日，两个办会

Located at the eastern end of Dingxianyan Village on Dingxian Ridge, the Niangniang Temple is one of the oldest temples in Suide County. According to an inscription, it originally stood in Yaoyanmao Village in Xianling Town, but was dismantled and reconstructed here during the reign of the Emperor Chenghua of Ming (1465–1487). The temple fair day falls on every 18th March. The main event of the Niangniang Temple Flower Fair is to present paper-flower trees to Niangniang. The flower fair proper actually lasts for three days, namely the 17th, the 18th, and the 19th of the lunar March, with the middle day being the principal focus wherein the main event takes place. Six clubs assemble the flower tree in rotation. Two of them collaborate each year so that their turn comes around once every three years. The fair events on the 18th and the 19th of the lunar March are organised by the makers of the flower trees. That held on the previous day is the responsibility of the He family of Dingxianyan Village.

The chief festivities are as follows. On 16th March, the two affiliation clubs and the He

事的社和定仙墕村何姓人家用唢呐鼓乐队把神羊迎到娘娘庙内，在娘娘的神像前举行领牲仪式；三月十七日，迎请诸位娘娘回归神位，享受善男信女的敬奉和香火，何姓人家将两个花树迎献到娘娘神坛前；三月十八日，由承办花会的社用唢呐鼓乐和八抬楼轿迎请娘娘牌位回自己的村子领受香火和观花。无论外村赶会的，还是本村男女老少，皆通宵达旦观花看秧歌，还要吃喝两天，求子的、治病的善男信女则在娘娘牌位前虔诚跪拜。第二天早饭后，迎花队伍伍簇拥着娘娘牌位穿山越岭走向定仙墕娘娘庙。迎花队伍除鼓乐队、仪仗队、彩旗队、娘娘神位楼轿、秧歌队外，还有五个高约五米的纸花树（每个花树由四个壮汉轮流举，

family will lead the sheep chosen and raised in the previous year into the Niangniang Temple with a band of *suona* horns and drums. There a ceremony is enacted in front of the statue of Niangniang and the sheep then become the divine sheep of the year to come. On 17th March, Niangniang will be invited to return to the "throne" to enjoy worship and incense offerings from devout men and women. The He family will present two paper-flower trees at the altar of Niangniang. On 18th March, the club (known in Chinese as *She*) that is hosting the flower fair will escort the statue of Niangniang siting in a sedan chair carried by 8 bearers back to the village she blesses to receive incense and flower trees together with the band of *suona* players and drums. Both visitors and local villagers will stay up all night to appreciate the paper-flower trees, watch *yangge* dance, and eat and drink for two days. People who wish to pray for pregnancy and healing from disease will bow down and worship before the tablet of Niangniang. After breakfast the next day, the flower-welcoming team will swarm around the tablet of Niangniang crossing the mountain and ridges to the Niangniang Temple in Dingxianyan Village. Besides the drum band, the guard of honour, the colourful flag team, the sedan chair bearing Niangniang's effigy and the *yangge*

并有四个护花人），五个花树五种颜色，代表"金、木、水、火、土"之五行观。迎花队伍到定仙墕街上后要游街一周，并举行赛花仪式，同时在挂塔渠挂起八丈长的五彩纸塔。这个过程最为热闹壮观，迎花队伍似彩龙在人海中穿行，唢呐、秧歌、大戏把仙岭古镇闹得红天火地。

随后，迎花队伍进入娘娘庙内，尊请娘娘回归神坛，花树在庙院内敬献10多分钟后，即焚烧于大殿前，随即举行迎贡、献贡、祭酒、收彩塔、焚烧等仪式。仪式举行完毕后，即交给另一个会社，筹办十九日的花会。十九日花会议程与十八日相同。

team, the flower-welcoming team also includes five paper-flower trees of about 5 metres high (each paper-flower tree is held by 4 strong men in turn and guarded by 4 people). The 5 paper-flower trees bear 5 colours, representing the 5 elements of "gold, wood, water, fire and earth". After arriving at Dingxianyan Village, the welcoming flower team will parade on the street for a week followed by a flower competition ceremony. At the same time, an 8-*zhang*-long (about 26 metres) multicoloured paper tower is hung on the hanging canal. This process is the most lively and spectacular part. The flower-welcoming group resembles a colourful dragon surging through a sea of people. And the *suona*, *yangge* dance and opera fill the ancient town of Xianling with excitement.

Later on, the welcoming flower team enter the Niangniang Temple and invite Niangniang to return to the shrine. The flower trees will be burned for more than 10 minutes in front of the main hall after being presented within the temple. Then, the follow-up ceremonies take the form of welcoming tributes, offering tributes, offering libation, collecting the colourful paper-towers and burning. After the completion of the ceremony, matters are handed over to another club that organises the flower fair on the 19th day of the lunar March. The agenda of this fair is the same as that on the previous day.

定仙墕娘娘庙花会迄今已有300多年的历史。定仙墕居于定仙岭上，山大沟深，荒凉恶劣的环境使得人们在大自然面前无可奈何。花会期间，五彩的花树，潮涌的信民，伴着吼天撼地的唢呐声，似彩龙缓缓行进在荒芜贫穷的仙岭上，把对生命的呼唤和生存的企盼，虔诚地托付于娘娘的佑护，娘娘成为当地居民的生命保护神。绥德定仙墕娘娘庙花会已列入陕西省第三批非物质文化遗产名录。

The Niangniang Temple Flower Fair at Dingxianyan has a history of more than 300 years. Dingxianyan is located on Dingxian Ridge. With such vast mountains and deep valleys, the desolate and harsh environment makes people feel helpless in the face of nature. During the flower fair, one can glimpse vibrant flower trees and enthusiastic believers accompanied by the roaring strains of the *suona*. It is as if a vivid dragon is processing slowly along the barren and poor immortal ridge. They devoutly entrust their call for life and their hopes for survival to Niangniang's care who is believed to be their patron saint to protect the lives of local residents. The Niangniang Temple Flower Fair in Dingxian Ridge, Suide was listed among the third batch of the Intangible Cultural Heritage in Shaanxi Province.

3.22 志丹过大年

Passing the Year in Zhidan County

过大年是我国最为隆重的传统节日，此习俗分布广泛。志丹过大年较为完整地保留了传

Passing the Year (Spring Festival) is the grandest traditional festival in China, and this custom is almost universal. The festivities for celebrating Spring Festival in Zhidan County retain

统习俗，尤以境内西川洛河流域年俗讲究多，内容丰富，最具代表性。过年习俗源自何时很难考究，不过一般认为起源于殷商时期年头岁末的祭神祭祖活动。农历一年的最后一个晚上，被称为"除夕""除夜""大年夜"，农历正月初一，称为元日、元辰。民国以来，把阴历的正月初一叫作春节。

志丹过大年特色鲜明。一是时间长：一般从腊月初八吃腊八饭开始，一直要延续到正月二十三燎干日结束。二是内容广泛：志丹过大年在漫长的历史发展过程中，吸收了全国各地许多古老的传统习俗，如拜灶神、扫除、祭祖、守岁、拜年、扫五穷、庆元宵等活动。三是充分体现地方饮食文化特色：志丹人过大年

their traditions in a relatively complete way. The practices in the Luo River Basin within Xichuan are the most representative, with complicated procedures and rich contents. The origins of Spring Festival customs are troublesome to trace back over time, but it is generally believed that they derived from the Shang Dynasty when sacrifices were made to the gods and one's ancestors at the turning of the old year into the new. The last evening of a lunar year, is known as *Chuxi*, *Chuye* or *Danianye* (New Year's Eve). Meanwhile, the lunar 1st January is referred to as *Yuanri* or *Yuanchen*, being known officially as Spring Festival since 1912 when the Republic of China was founded.

Passing the year in Zhidan County boasts distinct characteristics. First of all, its duration is particularly long. It lasts from the day when people eat Laba congee (rice porridge with nuts and dried fruit) on the 8th day of the lunar December to the 23rd day of the lunar January, the day when cooking wares and clothes are singed in flames, implying the burying away of disasters and diseases. Secondly, it embraces rich contents. In the course of its long evolution it has absorbed many ancient and traditional customs from all over the country, such as paying respect to Kitchen God, sweeping the house, worshipping one's ancestors, staying up on New

时要吃黄米馍、稠酒、小鏊馍馍、炸油糕、油馍馍等富有地方特色的食品。四是家家户户贴窗花。志丹窗花是当地人专为过年剪制的一种民间艺术作品。志丹窗花小巧、精细，内容丰富，形态各异，为过大年增添了节日的祥和喜庆气氛，表达了人们对美好生活的向往和追求。五是文化活动丰富多彩：从农历正月初三开始，农民们便自发地组织起秧歌队，挨家挨户去拜年（当地人称为沿门子）。当地的秧歌、鼓舞形式较多，其中志丹羊皮扇鼓尤其受到群众喜爱，这些异彩纷呈的秧歌活动从农历正月初三开始，一直延续到正月十五结束。志丹过大年体现的文化内容十分丰富，许多活动还富有浓厚的宗教色彩，如祭神、祭祖、祈福、辟

Year's Eve, paying New Year's visit, exorcising the five demons (evil things, monsters, disasters, diseases and poverty), and celebrating the Lantern Festival. Thirdly, it fully reflects the characteristics of the local cuisine culture. Such local flavours as millet steamed buns, glutinous rice wine, vegetable pancakes made on iron plate, fried glutinous rice blocks and fried cakes. Decorating windows with paper-cuts is the fourth characteristic for Zhidan people to pass the year. As a work of folk art, these tiny, exquisite window paper-cuts with rich contents and different shapes are specially-cut by local people for the Spring Festival. They add a harmonious and festive atmosphere to the festival as well as expressing people's wishes for a better life. The last characteristic is the showcasing of rich and colourful cultural activities. From the lunar 3rd January onwards, farmers spontaneously organise *yangge* groups and walk from house to house to pay New Year's visits (called *Yanmenzi* by local people). There are varieties of *yangge* dance and drum dancing, in which the sheep-skin drum is the most popular among audiences. Such splendid *yangge* activities last for 12 days from the 3rd to the 15th day of the lunar January. The cultural contents embodied in the Spring Festival in Zhidan County are conspicuous. Moreover,

邪除病等。志丹过大年已列入陕西省第三批非物质文化遗产名录。

many of the activities exhibit profound religious features, such as the worshipping of immortals and ancestors, praying for blessings, warding off evil and diseases, and so forth. Passing the Year in Zhidan County was listed among the third batch of the Intangible Cultural Heritage in Shaanxi Province.

3.23 沿门子

Yanmenzi (Door-to-Door *Yangge* Dance Team Paying New Year's Visit)

安塞县流行着一种独具地方特色的民俗文化活动，叫沿门子。沿门子是秧歌队挨户拜年演出时的一种民俗活动。每年正月初二开始沿门子拜年，直到二月二"龙抬头"结束。沿门子队伍由长号、大鼓、大镲、唢呐、秧歌、腰鼓、旱船、蛮婆、蛮汉组成，涵盖了美术、音乐、舞蹈、礼仪等民间民俗文化形式。

沿门子拜年前，先要敬神。陕北农村中每

As a folk culture activity with unique local characteristics, *Yanmenzi* is popular in Ansai County. It refers to a *yangge* dance group performing from door to door to pay their New Year's visits. *Yanmenzi* begins on the 2nd day of the lunar January every year, and ends on the 2nd day of the lunar February, the *Longtaitou* (dragons raising their heads) Festival. The *Yanmenzi* group consists of trombones, bass drums, cymbals, *suona*, *yangge* dancers, waist drum dancers, land boats, and clown actors. It covers many forms of folk culture activities, such as fine arts, music, dance and etiquette.

Before the *Yanmenzi* begins, people must first worship a deity. In northern Shaanxi, every

个村庄都有自己的神庙，或几个村庄共同有一座神庙，在庙会会长的带领下，各村由伞头和秧歌队组成的浩浩荡荡的敬神队伍到神庙召请神灵。秧歌队先在庙门外表演，待会长向神灵献供，焚香叩拜，祈祷风调雨顺，人畜平安后，秧歌队和沿门子队伍进入庙内进行"三参三拜"。参拜后的伞头和秧歌队的人就成了神的"代言人"，开始挨家挨户拜年祈福。沿门子的秧歌队一般由60~80名秧歌队员组成，按预先排好的顺序轮流到各村拜年。沿门子途中要打一种信号鼓，招引沿途观众，每到一户人家，先让打击乐队进院敲打，随后伞头和秧歌队员才能边扭边进入院内。沿门子队伍来到主家门前时，主人要在"土神爷"前摆上供桌，燃香献供，

village has its own temple or a temple is shared between several villages. Led by the chairman of the temple fair, a mighty group of worshippers, consisting of, stand-up comedians and *yangge* dancers, come to the temple to invoke the deities. At first, they perform outside the temple gate. The chairman then offers tributes to the deities, burns incense, and prays for good weather and the safety of people and animals. The *yangge* group duly proceeds to enter through to pay their homage. Afterwards, the stand-up comedian and *yangge* group become the spokesmen for the deities, and start to paying their New Year's visits from one house to another. The *yangge* group generally consists of sixty to eighty members, and they go to villages in a prearranged order to pay New Year greetings. They beat drums along the way as a signal to attract people to follow them. The percussion group is the first to enter through the gate and beats out a rhythm. The stand-up comedian and the *yangge* players are then permitted to enter the courtyard while dancing. When they arrive in front of the door, the host of the house will set up an offertory table in front of the God of the Earth, burn incense and make offerings. The *yangge* group is now permitted to worship.

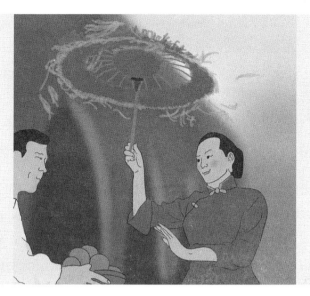

Pic. 39 *Yanmenzi* Illustrated by Mathew Russell

秧歌队要参拜土地神。

沿门子秧歌队要表演拜天地、大圆场、小场、大场等秧歌节目。伞头还要"出口成章",根据主人家的不同情况即兴演唱。拜完年后,主人送给秧歌队香烟、水果、瓜子之类,以表谢意。沿门子是陕北人民精神生活和情感的寄托,有利于维护社会的团结和稳定,具有重要的民俗文化价值和积极的现实意义。沿门子已

Yanmenzi yangge team bows to the heavens and the earth, forms a big circle, then a small circle, before uniting together in a grand performance. The stand-up comedian should adapt his or her vocal performance according to the different situations of the families the team visit. After the New Year's visits, the host will treat them with cigarettes, fruits and melon seeds to express his thanks. *Yanmenzi* exhibits the spiritual and emotional expectations of northern Shaanxi people. It is a form of social glue and an outlet for locals' souls and affection being conducive to maintaining the solidarity and stability of the society. Hence, it is of importance to folk culture

列入陕西省第三批非物质文化遗产名录。

and serves a positive practical significance. *Yanmenzi* was listed among the third batch of the Intangible Cultural Heritage in Shaanxi Province.

3.24 洛川婚俗
The Wedding Customs of Luochuan County

洛川婚俗既保留了中国汉族传统婚俗的主要特征，又具有鲜明、独特的地方特色。

拜双雁是洛川婚俗中必不可少的一个重要仪式。洛川人用拜双雁代替了拜高堂。"双雁"一般是在红纸上用墨或金粉写出相向而对的两个"雁"字，衔首交尾，周围饰以"牡丹富贵""连生贵子"等求子求福的吉祥图案，张挂于正堂，下置香案，新郎新娘对着双雁交拜，至此婚礼大成。拜双雁是古代婚礼用雁的遗风。《周礼·婚经》记载："纳采、问名、纳吉、请期、亲迎皆用

The wedding customs of Luochuan County not only preserve the main features of Han Chinese matrimonial traditions, but also display distinctive and unique local characteristics.

Bowing to *Shuangyan* is indispensable as a part of the rites in the wedding customs of Luochuan, which takes the place of the rite of bowing to parents. *Yan* refers to the Chinese character 雁 (wild goose), and *Shuangyan* means to write in ink or golden powder the character "雁" twice, one next to another, on red paper. Around the two characters are studded decorations of auspicious images with the connotations of praying for pregnancy and wealth. The red paper bearing the two characters usually hangs on the wall of the living room. Under the *Shuangyan* a table is placed for burning incense. The groom and bride bowing to the *Shuangyan* marks the completion of the whole wedding ceremony. The custom of kowtowing to the *Shuangyan* originated in the application of wild geese in ancient

雁。"是说婚礼除纳征（俗称过彩礼）外的其余环节都要用雁。婚礼用雁源于人们对鸟类旺盛的繁殖生育能力的无限崇拜及对爱情的忠贞不渝。大概是因为大雁不易捕捉，有的地方便代之以鹅，无鹅则用鸡代替。洛川一带订婚、商量话（即商定婚礼吉日）要用鸡，娶亲时亦须带一公一母两只活鸡。

洛川婚俗繁琐而隆重，尤其是男方家里，除婚礼之前的提亲、定亲外，在婚礼当日还有告祖、迎娶、闹洞房等礼仪。成婚后还要回门。

matrimonial customs. According to *The Rites of Zhou*: *Marriage* (*Zhou li hun jing*), a wild goose plays a conspicuous position in all six of the rites, excluding the presenting of betrothal gifts. It is involved in the remaining five, namely the boy's side sending a matchmaker to propose, asking for the girl's name and date of birth, the boy's side practicing divination to see whether the two sides match according to their dates of birth, selecting an auspicious wedding date, and wedding ceremony. A wild goose is used in the wedding ceremony because people wish to celebrate the fowl's fecundity and faithfulness in love. Wild geese are likely awkward to catch in some places, so a domesticated goose or even a chicken might function as a substitute. Chickens are used where geese are unavailable. For instance, chickens are used in the Luochuan area when two sides get engaged or select auspicious date. In addition, two live chickens, a cock and a hen, should be brought to the home of the bride's parents by the bridegroom on the wedding day.

The wedding customs of Luochuan are complicated and ceremonious, especially at the groom's house. In addition to the proposal and engagement prior to the wedding, other items of etiquette include offering sacrifices before the ancestors, collecting the bride on the wedding day, playing mocking games in the bridal chamber on the wedding day. After tying the knot, the newlywed couple need to "return home" (go back to the bride's parents' home).

洛川婚俗在民间代代相传,没有成文的规定,除遵从一定的礼仪和约定俗成的规则外,许多习俗都含有祈求早生贵子,促进家庭和睦兴旺等内容。

The matrimonial customs prevalent in the Luochuan area have been passed down from generation to generation but with no written rules and regulations. In addition to certain items of etiquette and customary rules, there are rituals by which to pray for having children and promote familial harmony and prosperity.

洛川婚俗从中国古代婚嫁"六礼"蜕化演变而来,蕴含着传统伦理思想和民族文化心理,具有重要的历史、文化和民俗价值。洛川婚俗已列入陕西省第三批非物质文化遗产名录。

Evolving as they do from the six rites involved in ancient Chinese marriage, the matrimonial customs of Luochuan embody both traditional ethics and modes of thought, thereby possessing important historical, cultural and folk value. The Wedding Customs of Luochuan County were listed among the third batch of the Intangible Cultural Heritage in Shaanxi Province.

3.25 陕北丧葬习俗

Burial Customs of Northern Shaanxi

目前,我国丧葬形式主要有土葬、火葬、水葬、树葬、悬棺葬、天葬、二次葬、衣冠

At present, there are nine recognised forms of burial in China, namely burial in the earth, cremation, water burial, tree burial, hanging coffin burial, sky burial (to let vultures eat the

3 陕西省第三批非物质文化遗产名录中的民俗
The Folk Culture in the Third Batch of the Intangible Cultural Heritage in Shaanxi Province

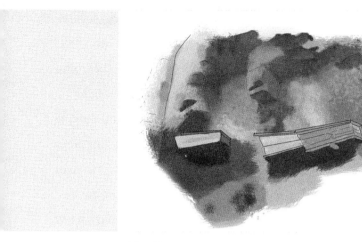

Pic. 40　Hanging Coffins Illustrated by Mathew Russell

葬、瓮葬等9种。而陕北的葬式就达8种，但至今最盛行的还是土葬。陕北丧葬（土葬）习俗，基本内容包括临终、倒头纸、挺尸、报丧、出讣闻、幡、棺材、戴孝、入殓、吊孝、迎客、上祭等30多项议程。

陕北丧俗既含有原始与封建的意识形态，又充分体现了传统的忠

corpse), dual burial, cenotaph, and urn coffin burial, among which eight can be found in northern Shaanxi, but burial in the earth is the most popular. The customs of burial in northern Shaanxi basically proceed in the following over thirty steps, namely, the death itself, relatives burning paper money for the dead beside his or her bed, moving the corpse to a hall, informing the relatives of the death, giving an obituary notice, erecting funeral streamers, preparing the coffin, wearing mourning cloth, putting the corpse into a coffin, offering condolences, receiving guests, offering sacrifices, and so on.

The burial customs in northern Shaanxi not only enshrine primitive and feudal ideology, but also fully reflect the traditional concepts of

孝观念,"孝亲"贯穿丧葬礼仪的始终。已出嫁的妇女死亡后,娘家人也要参与筹办丧事活动,并起着举足轻重的作用。从死者土葬地址的选择到埋葬各个环节的有序进行,阴阳先生都扮演着极其重要的角色。随着社会的发展,陕北传统丧俗已逐渐走向简约化。旧的观念意识也正在一步步被剔除,一种文明的丧俗正在由发达地区向欠发达地区逐步推广。陕北丧葬习俗已列入陕西省第三批非物质文化遗产名录。

loyalty and filial piety, which run throughout the funeral etiquette. When a married daughter dies, the family into which she was born also participates in organising the funeral and plays a pivotal role. A geomancer (usually employed as a funeral adviser) also plays an important part in the whole process, from the selection of a burial site to the orderly proceeding of the funeral rites. With the development of society, the traditional burial customs in northern Shaanxi have gradually been simplified. Primitive consciousness has incrementally given way to more civilised burial customs, which have spread outwards from the more developed localities. The Burial Customs of Northern Shaanxi were listed among the third batch of the Intangible Cultural Heritage in Shaanxi Province.

3.26 洛川灯会

The Luochuan Lantern Fair

洛川灯会,又叫灯棚会,是民间自发组织的为庆祝元宵节而举办的活动。每年正月初十开始做准备工作,如蒸花馍,炸油糕,搭建彩

The Luochuan Lantern Fair, also known as the Lantern Shed Festival, is a popular activity organised to celebrate the Lantern Festival. Preparations begin on the lunar January 10th, and include making decorated steamed buns (also known as courtesy steamed buns) and fried

门、牌楼、灯棚，家家户户扎花灯，等等。灯会从正月十三正午一时请神活动正式开始，到正月十六凌晨结束，历时三天。

洛川灯会分布在洛川县城凤栖镇的东社、北社、西社、东关4个社区。东社灯棚和西社灯棚供奉南海观世音菩萨。当地人视观音为送子神，因而观世音菩萨受到人们虔诚地顶礼膜拜。灯棚内神案后还放有"荞面"灯，供求子者索取。北社和东关社供奉财神。灯棚里有关公画像和塑像，两边有《桃园三结义》《刮骨疗伤》《封金挂印》等壁画。塑像前面的供桌上供有100盘色泽绚丽、造型奇异独特的面花，在彩灯的照射下更加光彩夺目。供桌的左面是"乐声家"（俗称"龟子手"或"吹鼓手"），由

cakes, setting up colourful gates, archways and lantern sheds. Every household is busy with making colourful lanterns. The Lantern Fair lasts for three days, from the activity of welcoming the deities on the lunar January 13th to the midnight of the lunar January 16th.

The Luochuan Lantern Fair is held at four communities in Fengxi Town, particularly the Eastern *She*, Northern *She* and Western *She* and Outside the East Gate. The lantern sheds in the Eastern *She* and Western *She* are dedicated to the Nanhai Avalokitesvara (Guanyin of the South China Sea), who is believed by the local people to be a child-bestower, therefore enjoys wide-spreading pious worship. Inside the lantern sheds a buckwheat lantern is placed under the incense table for people to pray for having children. The lantern sheds in the Northern *She* and Outside the East Gate are dedicated to the God of Wealth, Duke Guan, portraits and statues of whom are to be seen within the sheds. On both sides of the sheds hang murals of "Brotherhood Forged in the Peach Garden", "Scraping the Bone to Expel Toxins", "Refusing Bribery and Resigning from Office", etc. On the altar table in front of the statue are laid out one hundred plates of decorated steamed buns with brilliant hues and unique shapes, glistening under the coloured

唢呐、锣鼓队组成，右面是会长招待游客上香祭拜。在唢呐、锣鼓声中，关公像前焚香祭拜的游客络绎不绝。

洛川灯会除祭祀神灵外，另一个重要的内容就是观灯。其程序为正月十三"上灯"，正月十四"试灯"，正月十五"正灯"。在正月十三正午十二时前要挂好所有花灯。当地村民家家户户都要给灯会送自制的宫灯、转灯、鱼灯、莲花灯等各种样式的花灯，群众在观灯的同时还有灯谜活动及花灯评奖活动。有的社区还搭台唱戏，为灯会增加节日的欢乐气氛。洛川灯会已列入陕西省第三批非物质文化遗产名录。

lanterns. To the left of the altar table are the "vocalists" (commonly known as *Guizishou* or "the Drummers"). This group consists of *suona* and a drum band. To the right, the organiser of the lantern show will receive the visitors to offer incense. Amid the sound of *suona*, gongs and drums, an endless stream of tourists are seen to come to offer incense before the statue of Duke Guan.

Besides sacrificing to deities, another important aspect of the event is appreciating the lanterns. After two days' work on the lunar January 13th and 14th, all the festive lanterns should be hung up in appropriate places before 12 p.m. on the lunar January 15th. Lanterns displayed at the lantern show are made by every household. They come in a variety of shapes, including palace lanterns, rotating lanterns, fish-shaped lanterns, lotus-shaped lanterns, etc. While appreciating the lanterns, people can also join in the activities of lantern riddles and lantern competitions. Some communities also set up a stage for opera performance, adding a joyous atmosphere to the festival. The Luochuan Lantern Fair was listed among the third batch of the Intangible Cultural Heritage in Shaanxi Province.

3.27 扫五穷

Sweeping Away the Five Poverties

洋县扫五穷又称为"跑大角神",是人们用来求财纳喜、祈福禳灾、除瘟祛疫的活动,也是具有傩文化色彩的一种民俗事项。

扫五穷发源于商周时期,成形于唐代,宋时已经有了较为众多的扫五穷傩队诸神,明清时已非常流行,民国及解放初进入鼎盛时期。此后,扫五穷活动被明令禁止,改革开放后,扫五穷活动开始恢复。"五穷"即五个穷鬼,分别是智穷鬼、学穷鬼、文穷鬼、命穷鬼、交(结交、交往)穷鬼。到宋代,汉水上游的洋县民间将其演绎为钱穷鬼、粮穷鬼、寿穷鬼、吉穷鬼、命穷鬼等五个穷鬼。唐宋之时,洋县(旧称洋州)扫五

Sweeping Away the Five Poverties in Yang County, also known as *Pao da jiao shen* ("the God of Running the Big Horn"), is an activity to pray for wealth, safety and eliminating plagues and disasters. It is also a kind of folk custom with the characteristics of *Nuo* culture.

Sweeping Away the Five Poverties originated in the Shang (1600 BC – 1046 BC) and Zhou Dynasties (1046 BC – 256 BC) and formed in the Tang Dynasty (618 – 907). And there were already a large number of deities in the *Nuo* team of "Sweeping Away the Five Poverties" in the Song Dynasty (960 – 1279). It became very popular in the Ming and Qing Dynasties (1369 – 1912). Its heyday was during the Republic of China and the early years after the liberation of the country in 1949. However, it was banned by explicit order after 1949 and resumed following the Reform and Opening Up. The "Five Poverties" refers to five ghosts poor in wisdom, knowledge, literary arts, fate, and interpersonal relationship. In the Song Dynasty, residents in Yang County who lived along the upper reaches of the River Han developed its connotations into five ghosts poor in money, food, longevity, luck and fate. The

穷的民俗活动就已诞生，扫五穷傩队中诸神均为道教神仙，主神为法力高强的张天师，并有守门神及土地爷等角色。

每逢春节大年初五这天，扫五穷队伍成员便在凌晨四五点起床化妆，准备好各种道具。在化妆开脸前先要祭祀玉帝、地母神和龙神，有些地方也有敬唐明皇的。天蒙蒙亮时，扫五穷队伍开始游村串乡，许多乡间的扫五穷队伍甚至到数十里外的县城去扫五穷，活动一直持续到正午，偏僻山区则持续到傍晚。当活动结束卸装时，傩队须敬神、谢神。扫五穷队伍在清扫活动中一律不能说话、哼唱和嬉笑。扫五穷活动进行时伴有社

activities for Sweeping Away the Five Poverties in Yang County (formerly known as Yangzhou) were formed during the Tang and Song Dynasties. The gods in the *Nuo* sweeping team are all Taoist immortals, among whom the Master Zhang, a man with strength in magic, is installed as the main god, together with other gods, like the Guardian God and the God of the Earth, etc.

On every lunar January 5th, members of the sweeping team get dressed up at 4 or 5 a.m. and prepare various props. Before making up their faces, they will first worship the Jade Emperor, the Earth Goddess and the Dragon God. The Emperor Xuanzong of Tang (685–762) is worshipped in some places. The team begins to visit villages and towns at dawn. Many rural sweeping teams even go to counties dozens of miles away. The activities last until noon, or even evening in some remote mountain areas. When the event is over, the *Nuo* team must worship and thank God before removing their stage makeup and costumes. During the cleaning activities, the sweeping teams are not allowed to speak, hum or laugh. The activities are accompanied by a *Shehuo* performance, together with gongs and drums. When the team enters a courtyard, the gongs and drums are not allowed to enter but stay outside

火锣鼓。锣鼓不得入户进宅，只在户外助阵。洋县扫五穷民俗活动在全国独一无二，具有重要的历史、文化和科学研究价值。扫五穷已列入陕西省第三批非物质文化遗产名录。

playing with deafening sound. The activities for Sweeping Away the Five Poverties in Yang County are unique in China and thereby possess important value in history, culture and scientific research. Sweeping Away the Five Poverties was listed among the third batch of the Intangible Cultural Heritage in Shaanxi Province.

3.28 商南花灯
The Festive Lanterns of Shangnan County

商南花灯是流传在商洛市商南县的一种民间娱乐形式，是春节、元宵等重要节日民俗活动的重要内容之一。

商南花灯形式多样，内涵丰富，有"二十八宿灯""五行灯""十二生肖灯""八卦灯""太极灯"，也有人物、动物、花卉等造型的花灯。

商南花灯在表演时，常与狮子、旱船、竹马等项目相伴进行，

The Festive Lanterns of Shangnan County is a form of folk entertainment and also one of the important celebratory activities seen during the major festivals, such as Spring Festival, Lantern Festival, etc.

The Festive Lanterns of Shangnan County reveal rich and manifold elements in a variety of forms of lanterns, including the Lunar-Mansion Lanterns, the Five Elements Lanterns, Lanterns with the Twelve Chinese Zodiac Signs on, the Eight Trigrams Lanterns, and the Taiji Lanterns. There are also figurative lanterns in the form of people, animals, flowers, and so on.

The festive lantern show is often accompanied by other performances, like lion dance, land-boat dance, and bamboo hobbyhorse riding. With

场面壮观，气氛热烈。具有很强的观赏性，多年来深受群众喜爱。商南花灯已列入陕西省第三批非物质文化遗产名录。

such a spectacular scene and warm atmosphere, the event is marvellous to behold and has been deeply loved by people for many years. The Festive Lanterns of Shangnan County were listed among the third batch of the Intangible Cultural Heritage in Shaanxi Province.

4 陕西省第四批
非物质文化遗产名录中的民俗

The Folk Culture in the
Fourth Batch of the Intangible Cultural
Heritage in Shaanxi Province

4.1 蒲城芯子
The *Xinzi* Performance in the Pucheng Area

蒲城芯子诞生于唐僖宗乾符年间，兴盛于清同治年间，迄今已有1 000多年的历史。

蒲城芯子有单人背芯子和多人抬芯子两种。抬芯子以八仙桌为平台，以铁木结构的倒T字形的"根子"为基础，以铁制架子为托架，巧设机关，层层紧套，最高可套到3~4层、6~7米的高度。一台芯子上最多可上10余人，由五六岁的男女儿童表演。孩子们身着传统戏曲服装，手拿各种道具，被固定在高高的架子上，或站，或坐，或织布纺线，或旋转翻腾，惊险奇妙，煞是好看。蒲城芯子

The Pucheng *Xinzi* performance was born in the Qianfu regnal period (874–879) of the Emperor Xizong (862–888) of Tang, and flourished in the reign of the Emperor Tongzhi (1862–1875) of Qing. It enjoys a history of more than 1,000 years.

There are two forms of Pucheng *Xinzi* performance: back-carrying *Xinzi* (a villager actor carrying a steel prop with child actors from the village standing on it) and lifting *Xinzi* (several village actors lift a desk with child actors standing on it). The *Xinzi* is raised with the Eight Immortals (*Ba Xian*) Table as the platform, and the iron and wooden structure of the inverted T-shaped "root" as the base, and the iron frame as the bracket. The mechanism is cleverly designed and the layers tightly fitted. It can reach a maximum height of three or four tiers, amounting to almost six or seven metres. Up to a dozen of boys and girls (aged 5–6) can be fixed on the high frames made from steel. They are dressed in traditional opera costumes, holding various props in their hands, and adopt different postures, standing, or sitting, or weaving and spinning, or twisting and

扮演的大多是神话传说、民间故事、历史故事、戏曲故事中的人物。

蒲城芯子是集民间戏剧、音乐、舞蹈、美术、手工纸扎和锻造技艺于一体的大型综合性艺术和动静结合的立体造型艺术形式。蒲城芯子雅俗共赏，气势壮观，形态逼真，设计独到，玄妙刺激，令人叹为观止。蒲城芯子已被列入陕西省第四批非物质文化遗产名录。

flipping. The *Xinzi* performance is thrilling and wonderful. Most of the roles they play are characters drawn from myths, legends, folk tales, historical stories, and opera stories.

The Pucheng *Xinzi* performance is a large-scale comprehensive and multifaceted figurative art form replete with dynamic and static elements. It embraces folk drama, music, dance, fine arts, handmade paper crafting and forging skills. With spectacular momentum, lifelike forms, unique designs and breathtaking performing style, *Xinzi* performances prove both elegant and popular. They are suited to both refined and popular tastes. The Pucheng *Xinzi* performance was listed among the fourth batch of the Intangible Cultural Heritage in Shaanxi Province.

4.2 船张芯子
The Chuanzhang Village *Xinzi* Performance

船张村位于西安市高陵区崇皇镇南部泾渭交汇处的北岸，为古渡。船张芯子历史悠久，明末清初船张村已有芯子活动，迄今已有300多年的

Located on the north bank of the confluence of the River Jing and River Wei in the southern part of Chonghuang Town, Gaoling District, Xi'an City, Chuanzhang Village used to be an ancient ferry port. The *Xinzi* performance in Chuanzhang Village has been in existence for more than 300 years, stretching back to the late

历史。

船张芯子有一级芯子和二级芯子之分，现存的芯子以二级为主。二级芯子是在长方形木桌的中心，固定一根高1.8米的铁杆为芯，铁杆的上端左右方向以卯榫连接各种附件完成所需造型。表演时将9～12岁的男女儿童按所表演的内容装扮后，固定于各种造型的边角支撑杆上。船张芯子装扮好后最高处距离地面4.5米。由于船张芯子表演有伞尖上站人、空中吊人等技巧，加之人抬或车载时摇摇晃晃的动感，表演效果惊险无比。

船张芯子的表演分为人抬与车载两种，并有爬芯子、吊芯子、跪芯子、顶芯子、坐芯子、手撑芯子等表

Ming (1368–1644) and the early Qing Dynasties (1636–1912).

The Chuanzhang *Xinzi* can be divided into two styles: the first class *Xinzi* and the second class *Xinzi*. The surviving *Xinzi* mainly belongs to the second class. This kind of *Xinzi* consists of a 1.8-metre-high iron pole fixed at the centre of a rectangular wooden table. The upper end of the iron pole can be connected horizontally with various attachments with a mortice and tenon section to complete the required models. Then, boys and girls (aged 9–12) are dressed up according to the content of the performance and fixed on the corner support rods of various shapes. After the *Xinzi* is decorated, the summit of the rig is elevated 4.5 metres above the ground. Many skills are involved in this display, such as standing on the tip of an umbrella and people hanging suspended in the air. The performance is made all the more breathtaking by the shuddering motions of the persons or vehicle acting as the bearer.

The current *Xinzi* performance in Chuanzhang Village can be mainly divided into two forms with one people-borne and the other vehicle-borne. In addition, there are performance forms such as climbing the *Xinzi*, hanging on the *Xinzi*,

演形式。

芯子表演时，门旗在前，依次为2人执会旗、50人的仪仗队伍、30人的秧歌鼓队伍、60人的扭秧歌队伍、每桌4个人抬的芯子共8桌、30人的芯子鼓队伍、每桌4个人抬的芯子共6桌、车载芯子6桌、30人的芯子鼓队伍，每桌随行有两名持拐子的安全员，一次演出共需三四百人。船张芯子游演队伍气势宏大，锣鼓喧天，热闹非凡，具有很高的民俗价值和审美价值。船张芯子的表演内容有《黛玉葬花》《马踏匈奴》《三娘教子》《西游记》《断桥》《游西湖》《十五贯》《白蛇传》《李彦贵卖水》等传统戏曲中的精彩场面。船张芯子已被列

kneeling on the *Xinzi* and the head-supported *Xinzi*, sitting on the *Xinzi* and the hand-supported *Xinzi*.

The *Xinzi* performance takes the form of a pedestrian parade, with the gate flag leading in front, followed by two people bearing the club flag, the 50-member honour guard team, the 30-member *yangge* drum team, the 60-member *yangge* dance team, 8 tables carried by 4 people to a table, the 30-member *Xinzi* drum team, 6 tables of *Xinzi* each carried by four people, the 6 cars carrying *Xinzi* tables, and the 30-member *Xinzi* drum team. Each table is accompanied by two security guards with truncheons in their hands. A total of three or four hundred people are required for a performance of this kind. The *Xinzi* parade performance troops are grand and magnificent in scale, with gongs and drums, creating a boisterous and bustling atmosphere. It endows the *Xinzi* performance with profound folk and aesthetic resonances. The performances include many wonderful scenes from traditional operas, such as *Daiyu Burying the Flowers* (*Dai yu zang hua*), *The Horse Stepping on a Hun Soldier* (*Ma ta xiong nu*), *Giving Her Son a Lecture* (*San niang jiao zi*), *A Journey to the West* (*Xi you ji*), *The Bridge Cut Off* (*Duan*

入陕西省第四批非物质文化遗产名录。

qiao), *A Visit to the West Lake* (*You xi hu*), *Fifteen Strings of Copper Coins* (*Shi wu guan*), *The Tale of the White Snake* (*Bai she zhuan*), and *Li Yangui*：*The Water Peddler* (*Li Yangui mai shui*). The Chuanzhang Village *Xinzi* was listed among the fourth batch of the Intangible Cultural Heritage in Shaanxi Province.

4.3 二曲礼仪
Erqu Etiquette

二曲礼仪源于清初关中大儒李二曲的家乡周至县。二曲礼仪是结合周至的风土人情，将中国传统的礼节和仪式规范普及到百姓的婚丧嫁娶、寿诞、祭祀等民俗活动中的一种礼仪程式。

二曲礼仪在进行时设执礼者、受礼者、行礼者、仪注、祭品、祭文等。执礼者是礼仪的主持，负责唱读仪式，同时有礼宾，一般为二人、四人、八人，分别称启赞（礼仪总指挥）、通赞（负

Erqu Etiquette originated from Zhouzhi County, the hometown of Li Erqu, a great man of letters in the Guanzhong Plain (within the Passes) in the early Qing Dynasty (1636–1912). Erqu Etiquette is a kind of ritual procedure that draws upon the local conditions and customs of Zhouzhi to invigorate traditional Chinese etiquette and ritual norms in folk activities, such as weddings, funerals, birthdays and sacrifices.

Erqu Etiquette consists of an emcee, a recipient, a worshipper, ritual notes, oblations and orations, etc. The emcee is the host of the etiquette and is responsible for singing and reciting the ceremony, and there are several guests, generally either two, four or eight people, respectively called the *Qizan* (the chief etiquette commander), the *Tongzan* (responsible for the entire singing ceremony), the *Yinzan* (who

责全盘唱礼）、引赞（起引导作用）、哑赞（协助引赞并读祭文）。受礼者是指接受礼的对象，行礼一开始即要请出、安坐。行礼者指参拜受礼者的主角，行鞠躬或叩拜礼。仪注指的是礼仪的程序、仪式。

在行大型祭礼时，有严格的礼仪程序，要求行礼者祭前要斋戒、沐浴，行礼时要虔诚、心神专注，站立要恭谨，垂手弯腰，长幼有序，亲疏秩然，不得越礼。祭品是专门为祭祀神明而准备的，大型隆重的祭祀要牛、羊、猪三牲俱全，一般人家的祭祀只需备一只鸡和一大块猪肉即可。祭文即祭祀祝文，是拜祭神明时以言告神祈福致祷之辞，体裁分散文、韵文两种，极具感情色彩。

plays a guiding role), the *Yazan* (who assists *Yinzan* and recites the funeral oration). The recipient is the person who receives the ritual. He must be invited to go out and sit down at the beginning of the ceremony. The worshipper is the protagonist who pays homage to the recipient, bowing or kowtowing. Ritual notes refer to ceremonial procedures and rituals.

There are strict etiquette procedures for large-scale sacrifices. The worshipper is required to fast and bathe before the ceremony, and be pious and attentive during the proceedings, and to bend over with his or her hands down, to stand upright in order of seniority and affinity with no violation of the etiquette. The offerings are specially prepared for offering sacrifices to the gods. The grand and solemn sacrificial ceremonies require cattle, sheep and pigs. But an ordinary family only needs a chicken and a large piece of pork for the sacrifice. The funeral oration is a kind of a memorial eulogy to pray to the gods for blessings. The genres involved include prose and verses, with strong emotional characteristics.

二曲礼仪改变了以往礼仪的贵族化倾向，推动了礼仪的平民化，作为一种传统文化的载体，受到了广大百姓的欢迎。二曲礼仪已被列入陕西省第四批非物质文化遗产名录。

Erqu Etiquette altered the previous aristocratic tendency of etiquette and helped to popularise etiquette among ordinary people. As a carrier of traditional culture, it is popular among the general public. Erqu Etiquette was listed among the fourth batch of the Intangible Cultural Heritage in Shaanxi Province.

4.4 关中丧葬风俗
Funeral Customs in the Guanzhong Area

关中丧葬风俗礼仪分布在陕西省关中地区，可上溯到 6 000 年前的新石器时代晚期，那时生活在西安半坡的先民就有了一套属于自己的丧葬风俗礼仪。先秦时，丧葬风俗礼仪被列入"五礼"之中。

关中丧葬风俗礼仪程序复杂，礼仪繁多，主要包括以下步骤：小殓、报丧、奔丧、大殓、移灵位、披红、招魂、安神、三

Guanzhong funeral customs and rituals are distributed about Guanzhong (the areas within the Passes), Shaanxi Province. They can be traced back to the late Neolithic period 6,000 years ago, when the ancestors in Banpo (within modern-day Xi'an) had a set of funeral etiquette. In the pre-Qin period, funeral customs and rituals were listed in "the five rites".

Guanzhong funeral customs and rituals entail a complicated process, which mainly includes the following steps: dressing the deceased up in grave clothes, giving an obituary notice, relatives coming to pay condolences, the ceremony of laying the body in the coffin,

献礼、孝歌、奠酒、迎礼、扫墓、送葬、路祭、镇宅、净宅、下葬、祭墓、祭后土、谢纸、宴请等。

守孝三年期间还要进行以下仪式：打怕、伏二或伏三、过七、过百日、春分祭、十月一祭、大年三十祭、正月初一点干粮、正月十五送灯、中元节祭、周年祭、二周年祭、三周年立碑祭等。关中丧葬整个过程都伴着孝子的哭声，配以如泣如诉的唢呐声和有教育、缅怀意义的秦腔戏，能充分宣泄人内心的悲痛。

removing the memorial tablet, tying red cloth onto the shoulders of those filial to the dead when he or she was alive, calling back the spirit of the dead, pacifying the soul of the dead, offering sacrifices, singing mourning songs, libation, receiving relatives' sacrifices, sweeping the tomb, carrying the coffin to the graveyard, offering sacrifices along the route of a funeral procession, pacifying the tomb, purifying the tomb, putting the coffin into the tomb, worshipping God of Earth, burning ancestral money, and treating people with a post-funeral meal.

During the three-year mourning period, the following rituals will be carried out: *Da pa* (scaring away the ghosts), worshipping on the second or third seventh day after the death, sharing condolences and offering sacrifices on the following dates: the 100th day after the death, the vernal equinox, the lunar 1st October, the New Year's Eve, the lunar New Year's Day, the lunar 15th January, the lunar 15th July, the first anniversary and the second anniversary. A gravestone will be erected to mark the third anniversary. The whole process of Guanzhong funeral customs and rituals is accompanied by the wails and moans of dutiful sons and daughters, along with the sound of the

关中丧葬早期有土葬、火葬、野葬、衣冠冢、瓮葬等，现以土葬和火葬为主。关中丧葬风俗礼仪文化内涵深厚，以礼为先，孝字为首，仪式庄严，念祖怀情，为人生礼仪之最。关中丧葬风俗礼仪已被列入陕西省第四批非物质文化遗产名录。

plangent *suona* and the edifying and nostalgic Shaanxi Opera, which allows the bereaved to fully vent their sorrow.

There are many forms of burial in Guanzhong dating back to primitive times. These include burial in the earth, cremation, wildness (to let vultures eat the corpse), cenotaph burial, and urn burial (putting the corpse in an urn) in the early days. In the present day the first two are the main types practiced. The funeral customs and etiquette in the areas within the Passes have profound cultural connotations, with etiquette and filial piety forming their most crucial quality. The funeral customs and rituals are solemn, recalling the love of ancestors, and are regarded as the most important etiquette in life. Guanzhong Funeral Customs and Rituals were listed among the fourth batch of the Intangible Cultural Heritage in Shaanxi Province.

4.5 麟游地台社火

The Ground-Stage *Shehuo* Performance in the Linyou Area

麟游地台社火起源于明清，民国时期有了较大发展，当时几乎村村都有社火队。

The Ground-Stage *Shehuo* Performance (village actors performing in costumes on the ground) in the Linyou Area can trace its origins back to the Ming and Qing Dynasties, and

现在麟游地台社火主要分布在麟游县酒房镇、两亭镇、丈八镇和招贤镇地区。

麟游地台社火分文、武两大类。文社火又分唱曲和以丑为主的戏耍，其中唱曲现已失传。戏耍要求演员表演时既要活泼滑稽，又要有一套过硬的技艺，才能逗得人们捧腹大笑，百看不厌。武社火主要以表演杀战为主，套路有出场、杀战、进场等固定程式。

民间地台社火的演出及布阵吸收了八卦五行学说。演出时，观众围一圆场，如八卦中的圆，中间一堆火，四角各放四盏灯，象征五行，又代表五方五帝。人物行动有进有退，行走路线沿五行生克之线而运动，曲线行动路线

gathered force in the Republic of China period when almost every village formed its own *Shehuo* group. The practice in Linyou County is mainly to be found in the towns of Jiufang, Liangting, Zhangba and Zhaoxian.

The Ground-Stage *Shehuo* Performance in Linyou is divided into civil and martial varieties. The civil type features opera singing, which has been lost, and a clown show. The clown show requires the actors to be lively and comical with a fine array of skills which can hold the attention of spectators and make them laugh. By contrast the martial type is mainly about representing fighting scenes, which follows fixed procedures, including entering the stage, fighting and exiting the stage, etc.

The performance and arrangements absorb the theory of Five Elements and Eight Trigrams. During the performance, the audience forms a round stage, like the circle in the Eight Trigrams. At the centre is a burning pyre, with a light in each of the four corners, symbolising the Five Elements and Five Emperors. The characters pace forward and backward, along both the line where the Five Elements interact and the S-shaped curvilinear route, like the line

正如八卦中阴阳鱼所呈现的 S 形。

麟游地台社火属哑剧类形式，不言表，不说唱。演出形式分扎场和转场两种。扎场为在固定场所演出，多在正月初二、初三、初九、十五、二月二进行。转场演出固定在每年的正月初五晚上，叫作"踏五穷"。这一天，社火角子进入各家宅院，通宵达旦进行表演。地台社火演一个故事叫一"转"，长转可耍一个半小时，短转只用几分钟。脸谱分为大红脸、黑花脸、红花脸、净脸（文武）、丑旦（文旦、武旦）等。演出时，临场只需换胡须、把子（武器）、头饰。地台社火的服装道具为传统戏曲中的服装道具。伴奏乐器有鼓、小锣、唢呐等。

presented by the *yin-yang* fish in the Eight Trigrams.

The Ground-Stage *Shehuo* Performance in Linyou can be classed as a dumb show or mummery with no speaking and singing. The performance forms are divided into two types: *Zhachang* (performing in a fixed venue) and *Zhuanchang* (performing on different sites). *Zhachang* is performed at the following times: the 2nd, 3rd, 9th and 15th days of the first lunar month and the 2nd of the lunar February. The *Zhuanchang* performance is held every year on the evening of the 5th day of the first lunar month, called "scaring away five poverties"(those who are poor in intelligence, knowledge, literary art, fate and interpersonal relationships). On this day, the actors involved in *Shehuo* performance enter the house of every villager and perform from day till night. One story played in the platform *Shehuo* performance is called a *zhuan*. A *zhuan* in length (a long story) may take an hour and a half, while a shorter one only lasts a few minutes. Facial makeup can be divided into the following types: the red painted face (symbolising loyalty), the black painted face (signifying honesty and frankness), the *Jing* painted face (the civil and martial roles), the

演出的主要作品有《黑虎坐台》《伍员逃国》《破洪州》《保皇嫂》《三请诸葛》等百余转。麟游地台社火已被列入陕西省第四批非物质文化遗产名录。

Choudan (the female characters as civil and martial roles), etc. When performing, actors only need to change their beard, cold weapons and headdress. The costumes are usually seen in traditional operas. Accompanying instruments include drums, the small gong, the *suona* and so on. The main programmes performed number over 100, including *The Black Tiger Sits on the Ground* (*Hei hu zuo tai*), *Wu Yuan Flees the Country* (*Wu Yuan tao guo*), *Broken Hongzhou* (*Po hong zhou*), *The Empress Protector* (*Bao huang sao*), and *Three Invitations to Zhuge Liang* (*San qing Zhuge Liang*), etc. The Ground-Stage *Shehuo* Performance in Linyou was listed among the fourth batch of the Intangible Cultural Heritage in Shaanxi Province.

4.6 太白高芯社火
The Taibai *Shehuo* Performance on a High *Xinzi*

太白高芯社火是流传于宝鸡市太白县的主要社火形式之一。它起源于清光绪年间，当时大户王姓氏族每逢庙会或族中喜庆时为了气氛热闹，晚上打着灯笼进行表演，演

The Taibai *Shehuo* Performance on a High *Xinzi* is one of the main forms of *Shehuo* spread about Taibai County, Baoji City. It originated in the reign of the Emperor Guangxu of Qing (1875−1908). At that time, the Wang clan, a rich and influential family, performed with lanterns at night to create a lively atmosphere during temple fairs and clan

员随着锣鼓声边唱边跑圆场，当地叫"黑社火"。民国初年，族人王演在黑社火基础上添置头帽、衣服、把子（武器）等创办社火会，把黑社火变为马社火，由古装人物骑着骡马巡游表演。中华人民共和国成立后，当地百姓在马社火的基础上进行了创新，形成了现在的高芯社火。

太白高芯社火的制作需芯桩、抬杠、麻绳、芯杆等材料，其中芯杆是太白高芯社火中最主要的部分。艺人们运用力学原理设计芯杆，用来装扮各类造型的芯子。太白高芯社火多取材于神话传说、历史人物等，一般由2~4个四五岁的小孩扮演，演出前

festivals. The actors sang and ran around the stage along to the sound of drums and gongs. The local people called it "Dark *Shehuo* performance". In the early years of the Republic of China (1912－1949), the clansman Wang Yan added head caps, clothes and cold weapons on the basis of Black *Shehuo* Performance and set up the *Shehuo* Performing Society, turning the Dark *Shehuo* into the Equestrian *Shehuo* Performance, a kind of parade performance made up of figures dressed in ancient costumes riding on mules or horses. After the founding of the People's Republic of China, local people revived the Equestrian *Shehuo* Performance, thus establishing the current *Shehuo* Performance on a High *Xinzi*.

This *Xinzi* requires the following materials: a central pillar, carrying bars, hemp rope, and long sticks. The central pole is the most indispensable part of the Taibai *Shehuo* Performance. According to mechanical principles, artists can design and install *Xinzi* in various styles. The Taibai *Shehuo* Performance is mostly based on myths and legends or historic dramas, and similar sources. They are generally played by two to four children (aged 4－5). Before the performance, they are dressed up as characters from classical plays and stand on the

将他们装扮成古典剧目中的人物，站立在又高又细的芯子上，依靠底座中通出的芯子将孩子支撑起来，高悬空中并绑在芯杆上，一台芯子就装扮完成了。

太白高芯社火的整个芯子设计巧妙，具有高、悬、险、巧、妙的特点。表演方队有社火队和锣鼓队。其中社火队称为"转"，一般参与游演的社火为 12~15 转，一转 4~8 人，演出时间是正月十四至十六三天，内容以戏曲故事、历史故事为主，参演者大多为中青年，男女不限。太白高芯社火已被列入陕西省第四批非物质文化遗产名录。

high and thin *Xinzi*. The children suspended in the air are tied onto the central pillar from the pedestal, so that a *Xinzi* is completed.

The Taibai *Shehuo* Performance on a High *Xinzi* is ingenious in design, with the characteristics of being towering, suspending, dangerous, artful and marvellous. The performance formation includes the *Shehuo* team and the gong and drum team. Among them, the *Shehuo* team is called a *zhuan*. Generally, 12 to 15 *zhuan* participate in the parade, with 4 to 8 people in one *zhuan*. The date of performances falls between the 14th to the 16th days of the first lunar month, and the content of the performance is predominantly opera stories and historical stories. Most of the performers are young and middle-aged, being of either gender. The Taibai *Shehuo* Performance on a High *Xinzi* was listed among the fourth batch of the Intangible Cultural Heritage in Shaanxi Province.

4.7 华山庙会
The Mount Hua Temple Fair

自古名山都有朝山庙会。华山庙会于农历三月万物皆盛时节举办，取华山之神拯救万物、普降甘露之意。相传，华山庙会兴起于北宋，时有陈抟的弟子贾得升为纪念师父，于每年三月中旬在玉泉院设醮告祭，香客云集。此后随着民俗文化的发展繁荣和商贸活动的涌入，到明清时，这种民间祭祀活动就演化为万民朝山参神的民间庙会。

每年华山庙会开始后，就不断有大量信徒、香客来西岳庙、玉泉院等地上香磕头。庙会期间，西岳庙还

Since ancient times, famous mountains have held temple fairs. The Mount Hua Temple Fair is held in the lunar March when all new life is flourishing, implying that the god of Mount Hua has saved the world and is dropping the nectar of dew. Legend has it that the Mount Hua Temple Fair can actually be traced back to the Northern Song Dynasty (960−1127) when Jia Desheng held a sacrificial ceremony in the middle of every March to salute his master, Chen Tuan. The sacred ceremony attracted thousands of pilgrims. Since then, with the development and prosperity of folk culture and the influx of commercial activities, this folk sacrificial activity has evolved into a folk temple fair. By the Ming and Qing Dynasties, this civilian sacrificial activity had already evolved into a temple fair whereby millions of people made a pilgrimage to the mountains for worshipping.

After the Mount Hua Temple Fair is opened each year, a large number of believers and pilgrims come to the Xiyue Temple, the Jade Spring Temple and other places to burn incense and kowtow. During the temple fair,

要举行盛大的拜岳大典，玉泉院等道观、寺院也有参拜山神的活动。华山脚下人山人海，从西岳庙、云台观、玉泉院至华山南峰之巅，人流如潮，朝拜之人所施香资，足够庙院一年之用。

现在华山庙会活动内容更加丰富多彩，除有民间社火、秦腔演唱、素鼓表演等文化活动外，物资交流也十分活跃。1998 年，华山庙会期间，华阴市政府首次在西岳庙举行了规模盛大的仿唐祭山大典活动，吸引了数万人前来观看。目前，华山庙会已发展成为颇有影响的综合性文化庙会。华山庙会已被列入陕西省第四批非物质文化遗产名录。

the Xiyue Temple stages a splendid ceremony to honour and worship the deity of the mountain. The Jade Spring Temple and other Taoist temples, Buddhist temples also hold activities for offering sacrifices to mountain gods. The huge crowd that gathers at the foot of Mount Hua and the stream of people from the Xiyue Temple, the Yuntai Temple and the Jade Spring Temple surge like a tide to the top of the southern peak of Mount Hua. The money donated by pilgrims is sufficient for the temple to cover its costs for a whole year.

The activities of the temple fair are varied and vibrant. In addition to cultural activities such as *Shehuo* performances, Shaanxi Opera and the pure drum performance (a form of folk dance peculiar to Huayin County), the exchange of materials is also very active. In 1998, during the Mount Hua Temple Fair, a spectacular Tang-style sacrificial ceremony was held in the Xiyue Temple by the Huayin County government to honour the mountain. The event attracted tens of thousands of visitors. At present, the temple fair has developed into a comprehensive cultural temple fair with considerable influence. The Mount Hua Temple Fair was listed among the fourth batch of the Intangible Cultural Heritage in Shaanxi Province.

4.8 吴堡黄河古渡
The Yellow River Ancient Ferry in Wubu County

吴堡县位于黄河中游，晋陕峡谷西岸，县城东南边沿由黄河曲流环抱，形成总长47.5公里的黄河运输航道，主要渡口有川口渡、龟戏渡、下山畔渡等。

吴堡黄河古渡历史悠久。据传，中华人文始祖轩辕黄帝当年西渡黄河来到吴堡，并在吴堡传授农耕技术。吴堡黄河古渡文化包含渡工从起船到驶至终点全过程所蕴含的技艺和无畏的拼搏精神以及相应的渡河号子等。吴堡的每个渡口有四五名渡工和三四只大小不一的渡船。渡船为木结构，渡工根据客流量的大小选择载客的渡船。黄

Wubu County is located on the middle reaches of the Yellow River, on the west bank of the Shanxi-Shaanxi Canyon. The southeastern edge of the county is surrounded by the winding Yellow River, which forms the Yellow River Transport Channel with a total length of 47.5 kilometres. The main ferry services include the Chuankou Ferry, the Guixi Ferry, and the Xiashanpan Ferry.

The Yellow River Ancient Ferry enjoys a long history. It is said that the Yellow Emperor, the earliest ancestor of Chinese nation, crossed the Yellow River to Wubu, where he taught farming techniques. The ancient ferry culture encompasses skills across the whole process of sailing, together with the fearless fighting spirit of ferrymen and their sailing shanties. Each ferry at Wubu has four or five ferrymen and three or four ferry boats of different sizes. The ferry is of wooden structure, and the ferrymen select the vessel according to the volume of passengers. The current of the Yellow River is turbulent and waves come in torrents. In addition, landslips are common around the river channel as are shallows in the

Pic. 41   The Yellow River Ancient Ferry Illustrated by Mathew Russell

河水急浪大，加之河道中的滑坡、浅滩，行船时常常惊心动魄。渡工起船时喊着号子出发，行船中从不用帆，全靠老艄掌舵，小艄划桨，装卸货物全靠人背肩扛，如遇运送大牲口，则要事先用木板铺路。当黄河突发洪水时，渡工即使在洪水中行船，也能凭借丰富的经验战胜千难万险，确保万无一失。吴堡黄河古渡凸显了吴堡人民的聪

gorge. This makes sailing a thrilling experience. The ferrymen chant shanties when they embark. They never use sails for propulsion, only relying on the older boatman to manage the helm and the younger crewmen to row. The loading and offloading of goods are all carried by crewmen. If heavier livestock need to be transported, the ferrymen must pave the road with planks in advance. Even if the Yellow River is subject to flash floods or inundations, ferrymen who are in the middle of of a voyage can draw on their rich experience to overcome every difficulty and danger. Disaster can easily be averted. The ancient ferry service highlights the ingenuity and bravery of the people of Wubu.

明才智和英勇无畏的拼搏精神。

现今黄河大桥已建成通车，吴堡的几个渡口都趋于衰落。加之黄河渡工收入不丰，后继乏人，吴堡黄河古渡这一传统的民俗文化面临消亡的危险。吴堡黄河古渡已被列入陕西省第四批非物质文化遗产名录。

Now the Yellow River Bridge has been completed and opened to traffic. This has spelled the inevitable decline of a number of Wubu ferry services. Additionally, because of low incomes and a lack of successors, the traditional folk culture of the Yellow River ancient ferry is in danger of dying out. The Wubu Yellow River Ancient Ferry was listed among the fourth batch of the Intangible Cultural Heritage in Shaanxi Province.

4.9 柞水十三花
The 13-Blossom Banquet in Zhashui County

柞水十三花宴席主要分布在柞水县营盘镇药王村、朱家湾村和乾佑河沿岸的石镇村、石瓮村、车家河村、马房子村、沙坪村等地。

柞水十三花源于药王孙思邈创制的药膳。唐贞观三年（629），陕西耀县（今耀州区）神医孙思邈慕秦岭中

The 13-Blossom Banquet in Zhashui County is mainly held in the villages of Yaowang and Zhujiawan in Yingpan Town, Zhashui County, and the villages of Shizhen, Shiweng, Chejiahe, Mafangzi and Shaping along the River Ganyou.

The 13-Blossom Banquet in Zhashui County originates from the herbal food created by Sun Simiao, who has been hailed as the King of Medicine. In the 3rd year of the Zhenguan Era of the Tang Dynasty in 629, the

药宝库之名来到柞水，在县城北 10 余公里处的桦栎杷（今花里盘）采药、种药、制药。其时，当地流行小儿痢疾，药王把自己采集的中草药炮制后，用药和糯米熬制成食，装在 12 个盘子内，招来病童品尝。这些孩童吃得津津有味，很快病就治好了，遏制了时疫的蔓延。当地百姓感念药王的功德，就在桦栎杷下面建起了药王庙，将这个地方命名为药王堂，并用十三花席面纪念药王孙思邈，这一习俗一直延续至今。

柞水十三花宴席正式开席前有四荤、四素、四干果和一个"花开富贵"的拼盘，开席

highly skilled Sun, a doctor from Yaoxian County (present-day Yaozhou District), Shaanxi Province was attracted to the Qinling Mountain Range by its promise of rich resources for Traditional Chinese Medicine. He came to Zhashui County, where he collected herbs, seed herbs and pharmaceuticals at Hualipa (now Hualipan), more than ten kilometres north of the county town. At that time, infantile dysentery was rampant in Zhashui. After processing Chinese herbal medicine, Sun Simiao produced medicinal concoctions by boiling the medicine and glutinous rice, then placed them on 12 plates respectively, and invited sick children to taste them. The children tucked into them with zest, and this medicine has soon cured the infection and stopped the spread of dysentery. In order to appreciate and remember the merits of Sun Simao, the King of Medicine, the local people built the Yaowang Temple in the south of Hualipa and named it the Yaowang Hall. They also used the 13-Blossom Banquet to commemorate him, which has continued to this day.

Before the banquet starts, four meat dishes, four vegetable dishes, four dried fruit dishes and a mixed platter named "Blossoming" are served. When the banquet starts, twelve dishes

后要上四大碗、四大盘、两道衬碗、两道衬盘，共计 12 道菜，主要突出鸡、蹄、肘、肚四道大菜，并以蒸碗子为辅。接着还要上 13 道菜，中间还要加 4 道衬盘。宴席结束前上主食时，要撤下桌面上的 12 道菜，重新端上 4 个凉菜、4 个蒸碗、1 个汤，一般主食为米饭。柞水十三花做工精细，选料讲究，佐料配以中草药，具有滋补养颜、强身健体、延年益寿的功效。柞水十三花已被列入陕西省第四批非物质文化遗产名录。

are served, including four big bowls, four big plates, four small bowls and four small plates. Chicken, pig's trotters, hock and tripe form the main courses, and steamed bowls are served as a supplement. Then, another thirteen dishes and four small plates are presented. When staple food (here this mainly refers to rice) is served, the former twelve dishes are cleared, and four cold dishes, four steamed bowls and a bowl of soup are laid out. The thirteen dishes in Zhashui County are of fine workmanship and utilise high quality materials. Chinese herbs are usually used as seasoning. These help to nourish body and skin, fortify the body and prolong life. The 13-Blossom Banquet in Zhashui County was listed among the fourth batch of the Intangible Cultural Heritage in Shaanxi Province.

4.10 漫川古镇双戏楼庙会

The Twin-Theatre Temple Fair at the Ancient Town of Manchuan

漫川关位于商洛市山阳县东南，是明清时期重要的水旱码头，也是当时客商云

Located in the southeast of Shanyang County, Shangluo City, Manchuan Pass was a port city and a centre for distributing materials in the Ming and Qing Dynasties. Merchants

集的物资集散地。商贾们在这里先后修建了双戏楼、马王庙、关帝庙、船帮会馆、湖北会馆、武昌会馆、骡帮会馆等建筑物,并逐渐形成了规模宏大的庙会活动,迄今已有200多年历史。

漫川古镇双戏楼庙会兴起于清光绪年间,每年农历三月初三,附近的村民捧着香烛、供品,从四面八方赶来参加庙会。方圆几百里的人们也纷纷来到漫川祭拜祈福,寺院内击磬诵经,香烟缭绕,锣鼓喧天,鞭炮齐鸣,热闹非凡。双戏楼庙会的主要活动包括群众集体庙祭求福活动和瞻仰观光及文化、商品的交流活动。双戏楼庙会的宗旨是"合会共议,民主自由,一秉虔心,公益助善,自办庙会",

built the Twin Theatres, the Mawang Temple, the Memorial Temple of Lord Guan, the Chuanbang Guildhall, the Hubei Guildhall, the Wuchang Guildhall, and the Luobang Guildhall in succession here, and gradually laid out the format of a large-scale temple fair, which has a history of more than 200 years.

The Twin-Theatre Temple Fair at the Ancient Town of Manchuan emerged during the reign of the Emperor Guangxu of Qing (1875–1908). The temple fair is held ceremoniously on the 3rd day of lunar March, and nearby villagers from all directions are attracted to the ancient town of Manchuan. They carry incense, candles and offerings in their hands. People from hundreds of miles away also come to Manchuan to worship and pray for blessings. Within the temple, big mountain stones are beaten to the sound of scripture chanting. In incense smoke, the deafening sound of gongs and drums as well as the explosion of firecrackers create a boisterous and bustling atmosphere. The main activities of the Twin-Theatre Temple Fair includes the worship of gods, praying for blessings, sightseeing and cultural and commodity exchange activities.

体现了群众极强的组织协调能力。庙会期间商品交易频繁，有百货、山货交易，也有各种特色风味小吃供人们品尝。文化活动有大型社火、秧歌、皮影戏、自乐班演出和农业科技图书销售等。

漫川古镇双戏楼庙会保留了当地以民间信仰为代表的传统民间文化形态，是研究陕西东南部地区民俗文化的重要依据。漫川古镇双戏楼庙会已被列入陕西省第四批非物质文化遗产名录。

The purpose of the fair can be summarised as "collaboration, democracy, freedom, piety, devotion, self-funding", which reflects the strong organisational and co-ordinating abilities of the masses. During the temple fair, large quantities of commercial transactions takes place in a variety of goods and mountain products. Various special flavoured snacks are available for people to taste. Cultural activities include large-scale *Shehuo* performances, *yangge* dance, shadow puppetry, self-entertaining opera performance and the selling of agricultural science and technology books.

The Twin-Theatre Temple Fair at the Ancient Town of Manchuan retains the local traditional culture represented by folk belief, and is an important evidence for the study of folk culture in southeast Shaanxi. The Twin-Theatre Temple Fair at the Ancient Town of Manchuan was listed among the fourth batch of the Intangible Cultural Heritage in Shaanxi Province.

Acknowledgments

My first thanks should go to the project team at the Shaanxi Provincial Department of Culture and Tourism who compiled and published the original Chinese version of *Shaanxi Intangible Cultural Heritage* (Vol. 1-4). I owe my sincere thanks to Zhou Ying who works in the Office of Intangible Culture at the aforesaid department who helped in the authorization of translation. Without her help the publication of the English version would never have been possible.

I feel deeply grateful to my young friends who helped in supporting the research, the formatting of the parallel text, and draft preparation. Special mention should be made of He Jiale (Northwest University), my assistant in the office who helped with the draft of the third batch; Zhao Yingdi (Heyang Middle School, Weinan City, Shaanxi Province), who helped with the prototype Chinese draft which formed our manuscript;Zhang Hui (Zhengkai Middle School, Zhengzhou City, Henan Province) and Zhu Rui (Northwest University) who helped with the draft of the first batch; Wu Lingxiao (Ocean University of China) who helped with the draft of the second batch; Zhao Wanru who helped with the draft of the fourth batch; Zhang Yongying (Northwest University)and Zhai Heting(Northwest University) who closely read the publisher's proofs.

My special thanks are also due to Dr Robin Gilbank (Northwest University) who co-operated closely in the text translation and provided guidance and background knowledge in the illustration. I also owe my special thanks to Mathew Russell (Northwest University) who created the vivid original illustrations, vastly expanding his knowledge of local folk culture in the process.

The department also has my gratitude for years of encouragement and support. My supervisor Professor Hu Zongfeng has been my constant support and inspiration in my professional life. My beloved husband, Long, has been unstinting in his care and consideration.